SPIRITUAL

DISCIPLINES

FOR THE

CHRISTIAN

L · I · F · E

A STUDY GUIDE
BASED ON THE BOOK

DONALD S. WHITNEY

NAVPRESS
BRINGING TRUTH TO LIFE
NavPress Publishing Group
P.O. Box 35001, Colorado Springs, Colorado 80935

The Navigators is an international Christian organization. Our mission is to reach, disciple, and equip people to know Christ and to make Him known through successive generations. We envision multitudes of diverse people in the United States and every other nation who have a passionate love for Christ, live a lifestyle of sharing Christ's love, and multiply spiritual laborers among those without Christ.

NavPress is the publishing ministry of The Navigators. Nav-Press publications help believers learn biblical truth and apply what they learn to their lives and ministries. Our mission is to stimulate spiritual formation among our readers.

Printed in the United States of America

5 6 7 8 9 10 11 12 13 14 15 16 17 / 00 99 98 97

CONTENTS

THE SPIRITUAL DISCIPLINES... FOR THE PURPOSE OF GODLINESS

❖

Discipline yourself for the purpose of godliness.
(1 Timothy 4:7, NASB)

CENTRAL IDEA

The only road to Christian maturity and Godliness (Christlikeness and holiness) passes through the practice of the Spiritual Disciplines. These personal and corporate disciplines promote spiritual growth and have been practiced by God's people since biblical times. Jesus modeled them for us and expects us to pursue them. In doing so, we will taste the joy of a Spiritually Disciplined lifestyle.

WARM-UP

1. Describe a time when you disciplined yourself in order to reach a specific goal, or when you did not discipline yourself and failed to reach a specific goal.

What Is the Purpose of Spiritual Disciplines?

❝When it comes to discipline in the Christian life, many believers feel it's discipline without direction. Prayer threatens to be drudgery. The practical value of meditation on Scripture seems uncertain. The real purpose of a Discipline like fasting is often unclear.

It is said of God's elect in Romans 8:29, "For those God foreknew he also predestined to be conformed to the image of his Son." God's eternal plan ensures that every Christian will ultimately conform to Christlikeness. We will be changed "when he appears" so that "we shall be like him" (1 John 3:2). This is no vision; this is *you*, Christian, in a few years.

So why all the talk about discipline? If God has predestined our conformity to Christlikeness, where does discipline fit in? Although God will grant Christlikeness to us when Jesus returns, until then He intends for us to grow toward that Christlikeness. We aren't merely to wait for holiness; we're to pursue it. "Make every effort to live in peace with all men and to be holy," we're commanded in Hebrews 12:14, for "without holiness no one will see the Lord." This leads us to ask what every Christian should ask: "How then shall we pursue holiness? How can we be like Jesus Christ, the Son of God?" We find a clear answer in 1 Timothy 4:7—"Discipline yourself for the purpose of godliness" (NASB).

The only road to Christian maturity and Godliness (a biblical term synonymous with Christlikeness and holiness) passes through the practice of the Spiritual Disciplines. Godliness is the goal of the Disciplines, and when we remember this, the Spiritual Disciplines become a delight instead of drudgery.

God Commands Us to Be Holy
The original language of the words "discipline yourself for the purpose of godliness" makes it plain that this is a command of God, not merely a suggestion. Holiness is not an option for those who claim to be children of the Holy One (1 Peter 1:15-16), so neither are the means of holiness, that is, the Spiritual Disciplines, an option.

The expectation of disciplined spirituality is implied in Jesus' offer of Matthew 11:29—"Take my yoke upon you, and learn from me." The same is true in this offer of discipleship: "Then he said to them all, 'If anyone would come after me, he must deny himself and take up his cross daily and follow me'" (Luke 9:23). These verses tell us that to be a disciple of Jesus means, at the very least, to learn from and follow Him. Learning and following involve discipline, for those who only learn accidentally and follow incidentally are not true disciples. That discipline is at the heart of discipleship is confirmed by Galatians 5:22-23, which says that spiritual self-discipline (i.e., "self-control") is one of the most evident marks of being Spirit-controlled.

The Lord Jesus not only expects these Disciplines of us—He modeled them for us.

What Are the Spiritual Disciplines?

The Spiritual Disciplines are those personal and corporate disciplines that promote spiritual growth. They are the habits of devotion and experiential Christianity that have been practiced by the people of God since biblical times.

Whatever the Discipline, its most important feature is its purpose. Just as there is little value in practicing the scales on a guitar or piano apart from the purpose of playing music, there is little value in practicing Spiritual Disciplines apart from the single purpose that unites them (Colossians 2:20-23, 1 Timothy 4:8). That purpose is Godliness. Thus we are told in 1 Timothy 4:7 to discipline ourselves *"for the purpose* of godliness" (emphasis added).

On the one hand, we recognize that even the most iron-willed self-discipline will not make us more holy, for growth in holiness is a gift from God (John 7:17, 1 Thessalonians 5:23, Hebrews 2:11). On the other hand, we can do something to further the process. God has given us the Spiritual Disciplines as a means of receiving His grace and growing in Godliness. By them we place ourselves before God for Him to work in us.

The Spiritual Disciplines are also like channels of God's transforming grace. As we place ourselves in them to seek communion with Christ, His grace flows to us and we are changed. That's why the Disciplines must become a priority for us if we will be Godly.

The Fruit of Spiritual Disciplines

We must remember that the full-grown freedoms of discipline-nurtured Godliness don't develop overnight or during a weekend seminar. The Bible reminds us that self-control, such as that expressed through the Spiritual Disciplines, must persevere before the mature fruit of Godliness ripens. Notice the sequence of development in 2 Peter 1:6—"and to self-control, perseverance; and to perseverance, godliness." Godliness is a lifelong pursuit.

If your picture of a disciplined Christian is one of a grim, tight-lipped, joyless half-robot, then you've missed the point. Jesus was the most disciplined Man who ever lived and yet the most joyful and passionately alive. He is our example of discipline. Let us follow Him to joy through the Spiritual Disciplines. *(Taken from chapter 1 of* Spiritual Disciplines for the Christian Life.*)*

Persevering in the Practice of the Spiritual Disciplines
Three things, when understood, will help you persevere in the practice of the Spiritual Disciplines: the role of the Holy Spirit, the role of fellowship, and the role of struggle in Christian living.

The Holy Spirit. The role of the Holy Spirit is to produce within us the desire and the power for the Disciplines that lead to Godliness. That He develops this in every believer is evident from 2 Timothy 1:7.

The Bible doesn't explain the mechanics of the mystery of the Spirit's ministry to us. But these two things are clear: (1) He will be ever faithful to help each of God's elect to persevere to the end in those things which will make us like Christ, and (2) we must not harden our hearts, but instead respond to His promptings if we would be Godly.

Fellowship. No one should read of the Spiritual Disciplines and imagine that by practicing them in isolation from other believers they can be just as Christlike, perhaps even more so, than Christians who are active members of a local body of Christ. To measure progress in Christlikeness only in terms of growth in fellowship with God is an incomplete measurement. Spiritual maturity also includes growth in fellowship with the children of God.

Struggle. There is an element of struggle in Christian living. Many forces combat the spiritual progress of those still on this side of Heaven. Practicing the Spiritual Disciplines and progressing in Godliness will be accompanied by struggle. The victory that we actually experience over the forces opposing our progress in the Disciplines will come *through the practice of the Disciplines. (Taken from chapter 13 of* Spiritual Disciplines for the Christian Life.*)*”

Pondering Spiritual Disciplines
2. In the past, how have you felt about Spiritual Disciplines

such as Bible intake, prayer, worship, evangelism, and fasting? Be honest.

3. What single purpose unites the Spiritual Disciplines? (Colossians 2:20-23, 1 Timothy 4:8)

The Importance of Holiness (Godliness)
4. What does 1 Peter 1:15-16 say about the importance of holiness in believers' lives?

5. Describe a Godly person you know who has reached spiritual maturity through discipline. Which practical Spiritual Disciplines has he or she practiced regularly?

Catalysts That God Uses to Make Us More Christlike
6. *People.* Often God brings people into our lives whose input leads us to become more Christlike. Read Proverbs 27:17. Describe a time when God used someone to file away your rough, ungodly edges.

7. a. *Circumstances.* We've all faced trying circumstances that God uses to make us more like Himself. What does Romans 8:28 say about our difficult circumstances?

b. As a group, discuss how God uses circumstances in life to move you closer toward Godliness.

8. *Spiritual Disciplines.* Rather than externally coming from people and/or circumstances, this catalyst works from the inside of our lives and goes outward. Also, God grants us more choice regarding our involvement with this catalyst than with people or circumstances. Describe a time when God used your prayer time or Bible meditation to change you from the inside out.

Spiritual Disciplines:
A Way to Seek God and Know Him Better
Today people place great emphasis on physical exercise as a means of staying healthy. Spiritual Disciplines are similar to physical exercise, in that when we exercise ourselves spiritually we promote Godliness in our lives.

Let's look at two Bible stories that reveal how two people put themselves in the path of Jesus and sought Him. As a result, their lives were forever changed.

9. *Bartimaeus:* Luke 18:35-43
   a. What strikes you about his response to Jesus?

   b. In response to Bartimaeus' faith, what did Jesus do for him?

10. *Zacchaeus*: Luke 19:1-10
   a. How did this tax collector pursue Jesus?

   b. What does this story tell us about Jesus' mercy?

11. How do these stories encourage you to seek God?

The Spiritual Disciplines Are Like Channels of God's Transforming Grace
12. According to the text, as we place ourselves in the Spiritual Disciplines in order to seek communion with God, "His grace flows to us and we are changed." Describe a time when you sought God and His grace flowed into you and changed you.

The Lord Expects Us to Pursue the Spiritual Disciplines
13. What do the following verses say about what it means for each of us to be Jesus' disciple?

   Matthew 11:29

   Luke 9:23

   Galatians 5:22-23

The Consequences of Being Spiritually Undisciplined

14. Why do people who will discipline themselves for years to become proficient at their careers or recreational sports quickly stop pursuing the Spiritual Disciplines? Has this happened to you?

15. "The gold of Godliness isn't found on the surface of Christianity," states the text. "It has to be dug from the depths with the tools of the Disciplines." Think back on your activities last week. Were you able to use the tools of the Disciplines to dig for the "gold of Godliness"? If yes, what steps will you take to maintain your discipline? If not, what steps can you take to practice Spiritual Discipline this week?

Spiritual Disciplines Bring Freedom

16. a. "Freedom comes through mastery of any discipline.... The freedom of Godliness is the freedom to do what God calls us to do through Scripture and the freedom to express the character qualities of Christ through our own personality." In which areas of life have you experienced this freedom?

    b. If you haven't experienced this freedom, what steps will you take to bring yourself closer to this freedom?

Spiritual Disciplines Take Time

17. Read 2 Peter 1:3-6. Why must self-control persevere before the mature fruit of Godliness ripens?

God Invites All Christians to Enjoy the Spiritual Disciplines

18. When we practice the Spiritual Disciplines with the goal of Godliness in mind, our discipline has direction. Jesus is our example of discipline. Look up these verses: Matthew 4:2; Luke 2:46-47; John 13:2-6, 17:4. What does each say about Jesus and His pursuit of the Spiritual Disciplines?

Persevering in the Practice of the Christian Disciplines

19. Through the Holy Spirit, we have the power to persevere in the Spiritual Disciplines. Read 2 Timothy 1:7 and then describe why this truth should encourage us.

CLOSING PRAYER

Focus on God's deep love for you and on His desire to communicate with you through the Spiritual Disciplines. Ask the Lord to help you become willing to practice these Disciplines during the coming weeks of this study.

GOING DEEPER

(Extra questions for further study)

20. These days "denying oneself" is not a popular viewpoint. How does what Jesus said in Luke 9:23 relate to the practice of the Spiritual Disciplines?

21. Why is self-control one of the most evident marks of being Spirit-controlled? (See Galatians 5:22-23.)

22. What do you think the text means by, "The Spiritual Disciplines . . . are also like channels of God's transforming grace"?

23. According to 1 Corinthians 12:4-7, everyone has been given spiritual gifts. Why do you think Spiritual Discipline is so important in the development of these gifts?

24. What practical steps are you willing to take this coming week to begin building more Spiritual Discipline into your life?

BIBLE INTAKE (PART 1)... FOR THE PURPOSE OF GODLINESS

CENTRAL IDEA

No Spiritual Discipline is more important than the intake of God's Word. Nothing can substitute for it. There simply is no healthy Christian life apart from a diet of the milk and meat of Scripture. Bible intake is not only the most important Spiritual Discipline, it is also the most broad. It actually consists of several subdisciplines. It's much like a university comprised of many colleges, each specializing in a different discipline, yet all united under the general name of the university.

WARM-UP

1. Describe the Bible intake that took place—or didn't take place—in your home and church as you were growing up. Has that affected your view of Bible intake today? If so, how?

2. Have you—and your family, if you are married—developed a consistent pattern of Bible intake? If so, describe

the difference it has made in your life. If not, what keeps you from developing such a pattern?

The Importance of Bible Intake

"No Spiritual Discipline is more important than the intake of God's Word. Nothing can substitute for it. There simply is no healthy Christian life apart from a diet of the milk and meat of Scripture. The reasons for this are obvious.

In the Bible God tells us about Himself, and especially about Jesus Christ, the Incarnation of God.

The Bible unfolds the Law of God to us and shows us how we've all broken it. It also reveals how Christ died as a sinless, willing Substitute for breakers of God's Law and how we must repent and believe in Him to be right with God.

In the Bible we learn the ways and will of the Lord. We find in Scripture how to live in a way that is pleasing to God as well as best and most fulfilling for ourselves.

None of this eternally essential information can be found anywhere else except the Bible. Therefore if we would know God and be Godly, we must know the Word of God—intimately.

My pastoral experience bears witness to the validity of surveys that frequently reveal that great numbers of professing Christians know little more about the Bible than Third-World Christians who possess not even a shred of Scripture. We may nod in agreement that we must know God's Word intimately, yet spend no more time in His Word than those who have no Bibles at all. So even though we honor God's Word with our lips, we must confess that our hearts—as well as our hands, ears, eyes, and minds—are often far from it. Regardless of how busy we become with all things Christian, we must remember that the most transforming practice available to us is the disciplined intake of Scripture.

Hearing God's Word

The easiest of the Disciplines related to the intake of God's Word is simply *hearing* it. Why consider this a Discipline? Because if we don't discipline ourselves to hear God's Word regularly, we may only hear it accidentally, just when we feel like it, or we may never hear it at all.

16

Jesus once said, "Blessed rather are those who hear the word of God and obey it" (Luke 11:28). Merely listening to God-inspired words is not the point. The purpose of all methods of Bible intake is obedience to what God says and the development of Christlikeness.

One of the English Puritans, Jeremiah Burroughs, wrote in 1648 the following words of counsel regarding preparation for the discipline of hearing God's Word: "First, when you come to hear the Word, if you would sanctify God's name, you must possess your souls with what it is you are going to hear. That is, what you are going to hear is the Word of God." So hearing the Word of God is not merely passive listening, it is a Discipline to be cultivated.

Reading God's Word

USA Today reported a poll that showed only 11 percent of Americans—Christian and nonChristian—read the Bible every day. More than half read it less than once a month or never at all.[1] A survey taken less than a year earlier by the Barna Research Group among those claiming to be "born-again Christians" disclosed these disheartening numbers: Only 18 percent—less than two of every ten—read the Bible every day. Worst of all, 23 percent—almost one in four professing Christians—say they *never* read the Word of God.[2]

Since "all Scripture is God-breathed and is useful for teaching, rebuking, correcting and training in righteousness" (2 Timothy 3:16), shouldn't we read it?

Jesus often asked questions about people's understanding of the Scriptures, beginning with the words, "Have you not read . . . ?" He assumed that those claiming to be the people of God would have read the Word of God. When He said, "Man does not live on bread alone, but on every word that comes from the mouth of God" (Matthew 4:4), surely He intended at the very least for us to read "every word."

Here are the three most practical suggestions for consistent success in Bible reading.

First, find the *time.* Discipline yourself to find the time. Try to make it the same time every day.

Second, find a Bible-reading plan. It's no wonder that those who simply open the Bible at random each day soon drop the discipline. Inexpensive Bible reading plans are available in all Christian bookstores and in the back of some

Bibles. Or you may obtain a reading plan from your church.

Third, find at least one word, phrase, or verse to meditate on each time you read. (We'll look at meditation more closely in the next chapter.) Take at least one thing you've read and think deeply about it for a few moments. Your insight into Scripture will deepen and you'll better understand how it applies to your life.

Studying God's Word

If reading the Bible can be compared to cruising the width of a clear, sparkling lake in a motorboat, studying the Bible is like slowly crossing that same lake in a glass-bottomed boat. The motorboat crossing provides an overview of the lake and a swift, passing view of its depths. The glass-bottomed boat of study, however, takes you beneath the surface of Scripture for an unhurried look of clarity and detail that's normally missed by those who simply read the text.

Why do so many Christians neglect the study of God's Word? R. C. Sproul said it painfully well:

> Here then, is the real problem of our negligence. We fail in our duty to study God's Word not so much because it is difficult to understand, not so much because it is dull and boring, but because it is work. Our problem is not a lack of intelligence or a lack of passion. Our problem is that we are lazy.[3]

So discipline yourself for the purpose of Godliness by committing to at least one way of improving your intake of the holy Word of God—by hearing, by reading, by studying. For those who use their Bibles little are really not much better off than those who have no Bibles at all. *(Taken from* Spiritual Disciplines for the Christian Life.*)* 99

The Importance of Bible Intake

3. Do you agree that "there simply is no healthy Christian life apart from a diet of the milk and meat of Scripture"? Why, or why not?

4. How might your beliefs be different if you did not have a Bible? If you never received Bible intake?

5. Why is knowing the Bible intimately such a vital part of knowing God and being Godly?

6. The text states that we often honor God's Word only with our lips. In what practical ways might you add to that honor with your heart, hands, ears, eyes, and mind?

7. In our busy lives, it's easy to become preoccupied with "Christian" activities and not spend enough time in God's Word. What "Christian" activities are you involved in? In what ways is or is not Bible intake a part of these activities?

Hearing God's Word
8. Read Luke 11:28. Why do you think Jesus emphasizes this point?

9. If we aren't disciplined in hearing God's Word, which negative consequences will occur? Be specific.

10. What do the following verses say about hearing God's Word?

Romans 10:17

1 Timothy 4:13

11. What other ways, besides in a local church ministry, can you hear God's Word?

12. Why is it important to not be a "passive listener" to God's Word? How can you cultivate the ability to be an "intent listener"? Be specific.

Reading God's Word

13. Read 1 Timothy 4:7 and 2 Timothy 3:16. How much time, on the average, do you spend reading the Bible each day? Be honest.

14. What happens to a person who reads the Bible? (See Revelation 1:3.)

15. In the past, have you seen a connection between the time you spend in Bible intake and your knowledge of God and His power? Describe your experiences.

16. Why can Bible intake become a chore instead of a Discipline of joy? In what ways might meditating on Scripture deepen your appreciation of God's Word?

Studying God's Word

17. a. Consider Ezra 7:10. To which three key areas of study did Ezra devote himself?

    b. What did he do before he began teaching God's Word to the people?

18. In 2 Timothy 4:13, Paul asks Timothy to bring several items. What does Paul's request communicate to us about the importance of studying God's Word?

19. Do you agree with R. C. Sproul that laziness is the real reason why Christians don't study God's Word enough? Why, or why not?

20. What, in your mind, are the differences between *hearing, reading,* and *studying* God's Word?

CLOSING PRAYER

Focus on thanking God for sharing His Word with you. Ask Him to help you develop the Discipline of regular Bible intake so you can get to know Him better. Express your need for Him and His truths in your daily life.

GOING DEEPER

(Extra questions for further study)

21. If your growth in Godliness were measured by the quality of your Bible intake, how would you measure up?

22. What do you think Jesus meant when He prayed, "Sanctify them by the truth; your word is truth" (John 17:17)?

23. How does the emphasis of Philippians 3:13 apply to the failure many of us have experienced in daily Bible intake?

24. What can you do today to improve your intake of God's Word in the areas of hearing, reading, and studying?

25. Why is it important to continually receive Bible intake even when such intake doesn't emotionally uplift you or give you a sense of peace?

26. How do you think you'll feel when you finally see the Word of God in the flesh, in Heaven? How can this perspective encourage you in your commitment to know God more deeply today?

27. Consider how the following might enhance your study of Scripture:

- Writing down observations and questions about what you read.
- Looking up cross-references.
- Finding key words and seeing how they're used in other Scripture portions.
- Outlining chapters, one paragraph at a time.
- Doing book studies, character studies, topical studies, and/or word studies.

NOTES
1. Princeton Religious Research Center, *100 Questions and Answers: Religion in America* (1989), cited in *USA Today,* February 1, 1990.
2. *Bookstore Journal,* as quoted in *Discipleship Journal,* issue 52, page 10.
3. R. C. Sproul, *Knowing Scripture* (Downers Grove, IL: InterVarsity Press, 1977), page 17.

BIBLE INTAKE (PART 2)... FOR THE PURPOSE OF GODLINESS

CENTRAL IDEA

The intake of God's Word is the most important Spiritual Discipline. Only as we read and study the Bible can we appropriate what God has for us. We do this through memorizing and meditating on Scripture and by applying what we learn to our daily lives.

WARM-UP

1. How much time have you begun setting aside each day to read and study the Bible, as we talked about in the last lesson? What are you gaining from this time? Is this the right amount of time for you?

2. Which verses that you have memorized have special meaning to you?

Memorizing God's Word

❝Many Christians look on the Spiritual Discipline of memorizing God's Word as something tantamount to modern-day martyrdom. How come? Perhaps because many associate all memorization with the memory efforts required of them in school. It was work, and most of it was uninteresting and of limited value. Frequently heard, also, is the excuse of having a bad memory. But what if I offered you one thousand dollars for every verse you could memorize in the next seven days? Do you think your attitude toward Scripture memory and your ability to memorize would improve? Any financial reward would be minimal when compared to the accumulating value of the treasure of God's Word deposited within your mind.

Memorization Strengthens Your Faith and Ministry

Want your faith strengthened? What Christian doesn't? One thing you can do to strengthen it is to discipline yourself to memorize Scripture. Memorizing Scripture strengthens your faith because it repeatedly reinforces the truth, often just when you need to hear it again.

On the Day of Pentecost (the Jewish holiday being celebrated when the Holy Spirit first came to dwell within Christians), the Apostle Peter was suddenly inspired by God to stand and preach to the crowd about Jesus. Much of what he said consisted of quotations from the Old Testament (see Acts 2:14-40). Although there's a qualitative difference between Peter's uniquely inspired sermon and our Spirit-led conversations, his experience illustrates how Scripture memory can prepare us for unexpected witnessing or counseling opportunities. But if these verses aren't hidden in our hearts, they aren't available to use.

Memorization Supplies Spiritual Guidance and Power

The psalmist wrote, "Your statutes are my delight; they are my counselors" (Psalm 119:24). Just as the Holy Spirit retrieves scriptural truth from our memory banks for use in counseling others, so also will He bring it to our own minds in providing timely guidance for ourselves.

When Scripture is stored in the mind, it is available for the Holy Spirit to take and bring to your attention when you need it most. That's why the author of Psalm 119 wrote, "I have hidden your word in my heart that I might not sin against you" (verse 11). It's one thing, for instance, to be watching or thinking about something when you know you

25

shouldn't, but there's added power against the temptation when a specific verse can be brought to your mind, like Colossians 3:2—"Set your minds on the things above, not on earthly things."

Memorization Stimulates Meditation

One of the most underrated benefits of memorizing Scripture is that it provides fuel for meditation. When you have memorized a verse of Scripture, you can meditate on it anywhere at any time during the day or night. As you look for portions of Scripture to memorize, you might prefer to select verses on a particular topic where the Lord is working in your life right now. If your faith is weak, memorize verses on faith. If you're struggling with a habit, find verses that will help you experience victory over it.

Tips on Scripture Memory
A. Write out the verses on a sheet of paper or index cards.
B. Draw picture reminders to trigger your memory of key words in the verses.
C. Memorize the verses perfectly, word for word with each reference.
D. Find someone who will hold you accountable for your memory work and will review verses with you.
E. Every day, review some of the verses you have memorized and meditate on them.

Meditating on God's Word—Benefits and Methods

One sad feature of our modern culture is that meditation has become identified more with nonChristian systems of thought than with biblical Christianity. But we must remember that meditation is both commanded by God and modeled by the Godly in Scripture. So let's define meditation as deep thinking on the truths and spiritual realities revealed in Scripture for the purposes of understanding, application, and prayer. The kind of meditation encouraged in the Bible differs from other kinds of meditation in several ways.

While some advocate a kind of meditation in which you do your best to empty your mind, Christian meditation involves filling your mind with God and truth.

For some, meditation is an attempt to achieve complete

mental passivity, but biblical meditation requires constructive mental activity. Worldly meditation employs visualization techniques intended to "create your own reality," and while Christian history has always had a place for the sanctified use of our God-given imagination in meditation, imagination is our servant to help us meditate on things that are true (Philippians 4:8). Furthermore, we link meditation with prayer to God and responsible, Spirit-filled human action to effect changes.

How then do we meditate Christianly?

- Select an appropriate passage and choose the verse(s), phrase(s), or word(s) that impresses you most.
- Repeat each verse or passage in different ways, emphasizing different words each time. Think deeply on the truth that flashes into your mind each time you repeat it.
- Rewrite the verse or passage in your own words.
- Ask yourself questions about the verse or passage. (Does it reveal something about God? Something you should pray about or make a decision about? Something you should do for the sake of Christ, others, or yourself? And so on.)
- Ask yourself what God would have you do as a result of your encounter with this part of His Word. After your meditation, you should be able to name one (or more) definite response(s) or action(s) you will make because of what you have read.
- Pray as you read through the text. This will submit your mind to the Holy Spirit's illumination and intensify your spiritual perception.
- Don't rush through the biblical text. Read less Scripture, if necessary, in order to have adequate time for meditation.

The Value of Applying God's Word
The Bible promises the blessing of God on those who apply the Word of God to their lives. The classic New Covenant statement on the value of integrating the spiritual with the concrete is James 1:22-25. Pithy and powerful is Jesus' similar statement, "Now that you know these things, you will be blessed if you do them" (John 13:17).

Despite the difficulty and spiritual opposition, are you

willing, at all costs, to begin using your mind "in a disciplined way" to feed on the Word of God "for the purpose of Godliness"? *(Taken from chapter 3 of* Spiritual Disciplines for the Christian Life.*)*"

Exploring Scripture Memorization

3. How does Jesus' confrontation with Satan (Matthew 4:1-11) illustrate the power of Scripture that is committed to memory?

4. Read Proverbs 22:17-19. Why should we keep God's Word within us and ready on our lips?

5. Describe a time, if you can, when Scripture memory helped you during a witnessing or counseling opportunity. Share your experience with the group.

6. What does Psalm 119:24 say about guidance? How might you apply this truth to your busy life?

7. What was the psalmist's attitude toward Scripture? (See Psalm 119:97.)

Exploring Biblical Meditation

8. Name several differences between biblical meditation and other kinds of meditation.

9. Read Joshua 1:8. What did God command Joshua to do, and what did God promise would happen as a result of Joshua's obedience?

10. What do you think it means to meditate on God's Word throughout the day and night?

11. Which aspects of daily life distract you from concentrating your thoughts on God and His wisdom, and what will you do to overcome these distractions?

12. As we meditate on Scripture, what happens to our minds? (See Romans 12:2.)

Applying God's Word to Our Daily Lives
13. Read James 1:22-25. When you read the Bible, do you find it easy to apply what you read to your life? Why, or why not?

14. a. Sometimes Christians use verses incorrectly to try to prove a certain point. Why is it so important for people to understand the meaning of particular verses in context before applying the verses to their lives?

b. Why is an overall intake of Scripture through hearing, reading, and studying the Bible so important?

15. Consider this statement: "Biblical meditation isn't an end in itself; it is the key to putting the truths and realities of Scripture into practice." Do you agree? Why, or why not?

16. What steps will you take to deal with the obstacles you expect to face as you begin to memorize God's Word?

17. What three steps can you take this week to cultivate the Discipline of meditating on God's Word?

CLOSING PRAYER

Ask God to open your eyes and show you the wonderful truths in His Word. Praise Him for who He is and ask Him to guide you as you seek to apply biblical truths in your life this coming week.

GOING DEEPER
(Extra questions for further study)

18. List several of your concerns and personal needs. Find verses that apply to each concern and need and memorize them before next week's meeting.

19. The Bible refers to four general objects of meditation:
(1) the content of Scripture, (2) God's creation, (3) God's
providence, and (4) God's character. Using the following
chart, write down specific objects of meditation found in
each of these verses:

God's Word:	Joshua 1:8	
	Psalm 1:2	
	Psalm 119:15 (two objects here)	
	Psalm 119:23	
	Psalm 119:48	
	Psalm 119:78	
	Psalm 119:97	
	Psalm 119:99	
	Psalm 119:148	
God's Creation	Psalm 143:5	
God's Providence	Psalm 77:12 (two objects here)	
	Psalm 119:27	
	Psalm 143:5	
	Psalm 145:5	
God's Character	Psalm 63:6	
	Psalm 145:5	

PRAYER...FOR THE PURPOSE OF GODLINESS

CENTRAL IDEA
Prayer is a vital Spiritual Discipline, second only to the intake of God's Word. To be like Jesus, we must pray. Knowing that without prayer we will lack Godliness, God expects us to pray. What a blessing it is to know that He hears every prayer of His children.

WARM-UP
1. It is believed that many Christians pray less than seven minutes daily, even though they know that prayer is a vital Christian Discipline. Why might this be so?

2. How do you know when you haven't been praying enough? What are your feelings and concerns during those times?

Prayer Is Expected
❝I realize that to say prayer is expected of us may make the children of a nonconformist, anti-authoritarian age bristle a

bit. Those who have been brought under the authority of Christ and the Bible, however, know that the will of God is for us to pray. But we also believe that His will is good. Furthermore, it is a Person, the Lord Jesus Christ, with all authority and with all love, who expects us to pray. These excerpts from His words show that He Himself expects us to pray:

> Matthew 6:5—"And when you pray...."
> Matthew 6:6—"But when you pray...."
> Matthew 6:7—"And when you pray...."
> Matthew 6:9—"This ... is how you should pray...."
> Luke 11:9—"Ask ... ; seek ... ; knock."

The Expectation Is Specific
Colossians 4:2 says, "Devote yourselves to prayer." Everyone is devoted to something. Most of us are devoted to many things. When you make something a priority, when you will sacrifice for it, when you will give time to it, you know you are devoted to it. God expects Christians to be devoted to prayer.

First Thessalonians 5:17 states, "Pray continually." While "devote yourselves to prayer" emphasizes prayer as an activity, "pray continually" reminds us that prayer is also a relationship. Prayer is in one sense an expression of a Christian's unbroken relationship with the Father. So we must see the expectation to pray not only as a divine summons, but also as a royal invitation. As the writer of Hebrews tells us, "Let us then approach the throne of grace with confidence, so that we may receive mercy and find grace to help us in our time of need" (4:16).

God also expects us to pray just as a general expects to hear from his soldiers in the battle. One writer reminds us that "prayer is a walkie-talkie for warfare, not a domestic intercom for increasing our conveniences."[1] God expects us to use the walkie-talkie of prayer because that is the means He has ordained not only for Godliness, but also for the spiritual warfare between His Kingdom and the kingdom of His Enemy. To abandon prayer is to fight the battle with our own resources at best, and to lose interest in the battle at worst.

This much we know—Jesus prayed. Luke tells us, "But Jesus often withdrew to lonely places and prayed" (Luke

5:16). If Jesus needed to pray, how much more do we need to pray? Continual prayer is expected of us because we need it.

Why, then, do so many believers confess that they do not pray as they should? Sometimes the problem is primarily a lack of discipline. Prayer is never planned; time is never allotted just for praying. Often we do not pray because we doubt that anything will actually happen if we pray. Of course, we don't admit this publicly. A lack of sensing the nearness of God may also discourage prayer. When there is little awareness of real need there is little real prayer. Some circumstances drive us to our knees. But there are periods when life seems quite manageable. Although Jesus said, "Apart from me you can do nothing" (John 15:5), this truth hits home more forcefully at some times than at others. When our awareness of the greatness of God and the gospel is dim, our prayer lives will be small. Another reason many Christians pray so little is because they haven't learned about prayer.

Prayer Is Learned
There is a sense in which prayer needs to be taught to a child of God no more than a baby needs to be taught to cry. But crying for basic needs is minimal communication, and we must soon grow beyond that infancy. The Bible says we must pray for the glory of God, in His will, in faith, in the name of Jesus, with persistence, and more. A child of God gradually learns to pray like this in the same way that a growing child learns to talk. Note the ways we learn how to pray.

By praying. If you've ever learned a foreign language, you know that you learn it best when you actually have to speak it. The same is true with the "foreign language" of prayer. The best way to learn how to pray is to pray.

By meditating on Scripture. Meditation is the missing link between Bible intake and prayer. The two are often disjointed when they should be united. At least two Scriptures plainly teach this by example. David prayed in Psalm 5:1, "Give ear to my words, O LORD, consider my sighing." The Hebrew word rendered as "sighing" may also be translated "meditation." In fact, this same word is used with that meaning in another passage, Psalm 19:14—"May the words of my mouth and the meditation of my heart be pleasing in your sight, O Lord, my Rock and my Redeemer." Notice that both

34

verses are prayers and both refer to other "words" spoken in prayer. Yet in each case meditation was a catalyst that catapulted David from the truth of God into talking with God.

The process works like this: After the input of a passage of Scripture, meditation allows us to take what God has said to us and think deeply on it, digest it, and then speak to God about it in meaningful prayer. As a result, we pray about what we've encountered in the Bible, now personalized through meditation. And not only do we have something substantial to say in prayer, and the confidence that we are praying God's thoughts to Him, but we can transition smoothly into prayer with a passion for what we're praying about.

William Bates, called "that most classic and cultured of the later Puritan preachers," said, "What is the reason that our desires like an arrow shot by a weak bow do not reach the mark? But only this, we do not meditate before prayer. . . . The great reason why our prayers are ineffectual, is because we do not meditate before them."[2]

By praying with others. The disciples learned to pray not only by hearing Jesus teach about prayer, but also by being with Him when He prayed. In a similar way, we can learn to pray by praying with other people who can model true prayer for us. But we pray with them to learn principles of prayer, not phrases for prayer.

By reading about prayer. Reading about prayer instead of praying simply will not do. But reading about prayer *in addition to* prayer can be a valuable way to learn. Reading the books of wise men and women of prayer gives us the privilege of "walking" with them and learning the insights God gave them on how to pray.

Let me add a word of encouragement. No matter how difficult prayer is for you, if you will persevere in learning how to pray you will always have the hope of an even stronger and more fruitful prayer life ahead of you.

Prayer Is Answered

I love how David addresses the Lord in Psalm 65:2—"O you who hear prayer." Perhaps no principle of prayer is more taken for granted than this one—that prayer is answered. Try to read this promise of Jesus as though it were for the first time: "Ask and it will be given to you; seek and you will find; knock and the door will be opened to you. For everyone who asks receives; he who seeks finds; and to him who knocks, the door will be opened" (Matthew 7:7-8). Since God answers prayer, when we "ask and receive not" we must consider the possibility that something is amiss or wanting in our prayer.

God doesn't mock us with His promises to answer prayer. He does not lead us to pray in order to frustrate us by slamming Heaven's door in our face. Let's discipline ourselves to pray and to learn about prayer so that we may be more like Jesus in experiencing the joy of answered prayer.

Men and women of God are always men and women of prayer. My pastoral experience concurs with the words of J. C. Ryle: "I believe that those who are not eminently holy pray *little*, and those who are eminently holy pray *much*."[3] Would you be like Christ? Then do as He did—discipline yourself to be a person of prayer. *(Taken from chapter 4 of* Spiritual Disciplines for the Christian Life.)**

God Expects Us to Pray

3. What do these verses teach about Jesus' view of prayer? (Matthew 6:5-7,9; Luke 11:9, 18:1)

4. How might you apply Colossians 4:2 and 1 Thessalonians 5:17 in the midst of your busy schedule?

5. When we don't speak with a friend for quite a while, it's difficult to know how he or she is doing. Might we compare our prayers to God with communication with a friend? If so, explain. If not, why not?

6. Have you ever felt that prayer was more *obligation* than *opportunity*? If so, why? If not, why not?

7. Why did Jesus pray in "lonely places"? (Luke 5:16)

8. Describe a time when God answered your specific prayer.

9. Why should our praying be governed by the truth of Scripture rather than by our feelings?

Prayer Is Learned

10. Has anyone ever taught you about prayer? If so, who? If not, who might you seek out to teach you?

11. What role, according to John 16:13, does the Holy Spirit play in your prayer life?

12. How would you describe the relationship between biblical meditation and prayer? (See Psalm 5:1, 19:14, and reread the quote by William Bates.)

13. a. Thomas Manton, a Puritan preacher, wrote, "It is rash-
ness to pray and not to meditate. What we take in by
the word we digest by meditation and let out by
prayer." What is your response to this thought?

b. Why do you think more churches today don't teach
about the relationship between meditation and prayer?

c. How has this lack of teaching affected the Church as a
whole? Your life? The lives of others you know?

14. What is the difference between learning "principles of
prayer" and learning "phrases for prayer"?

15. What book(s) on prayer have you or others in the group
found helpful? In what ways?

God Answers Prayer
16. Read Matthew 7:7-8 again. Discuss the following phrases:

- Ask—and it will be given to you.
- Seek—and you will find.
- Knock—and the door will be opened to you.
- Everyone who asks—receives.
- He who seeks—finds.
- To him who knocks—the door will be opened.

17. a. Andrew Murray once wrote, "If you ask and receive not, it must be because there is something amiss or wanting in the prayer." Do you agree with this statement? Explain.

b. Discuss how the following may affect answers to prayer:

- Impatience/lack of perseverance in prayer.
- Selfish motives.
- Unrepentant sin in your life.
- Unwillingness to accept that God may answer in ways that are not obvious.
- Asking for things that are outside the will of God or don't glorify Him.

CLOSING PRAYER

Thank the Lord that He not only hears your prayers but also desires them because He longs to develop a deeper relationship with you. Ask Him to draw you deeper into disciplined prayer, to teach you what it means to "pray continually," and to show you how biblical meditation can strengthen your Bible intake and prayers.

GOING DEEPER
(Extra questions for further study)

18. a. At which times in your life have you felt that prayer didn't work, that God wasn't listening?

b. How does what you've learned in this session relate to this situation?

19. Does persistent prayer tend to develop deeper gratitude toward God? Faith in God? Explain your answer. (See Matthew 7:7-8, Luke 18:1-8.)

20. In what ways does the Enemy sidetrack your prayer life? Be specific.

21. What do you think is the relationship between a Christian's view of God's willingness and ability to answer prayer, the person's love for God, and his or her willingness to persevere in prayer?

22. Think about a time when you experienced the joy of answered prayer. What did you learn during that time that you might apply to your situation today?

23. If we do not persevere in prayer, what are we demonstrating that we believe about God's love for us? About His promises to us?

24. This week, plan to link your Bible reading to prayer through biblical meditation. Share your experiences with the group when you meet again.

NOTES
1. From the book *Desiring God: Meditations of a Christian Hedonist* by John Piper, copyright 1986 by Multnomah Press. Published by Multnomah Press, Portland, Oregon 97266. Used by permission, page 147.
2. William Bates, *The Whole Works of the Rev. W. Bates*, arr. and rev. W. Farmer (Harrisburg, PA: Sprinkle, 1990, reprint), vol. 3, page 130.
3. J. C. Ryle, *A Call to Prayer* (Grand Rapids, MI: Baker Book House, 1979), page 35.

WORSHIP...FOR THE PURPOSE OF GODLINESS

❖

"Worship the Lord your God."
(Matthew 4:10)

CENTRAL IDEA

Worship—focusing on and responding to God—is the duty and privilege of all people. Worship often includes words and actions but goes beyond them to the focus of our hearts and minds. God expects us to worship Him, our Creator, in Spirit and according to the truth of Scripture. We cannot become Godly without worshiping Him, but it is possible to worship Him in vain (Matthew 15:8-9). As we learn the Spiritual Discipline of worship, we will become more like Jesus and understand and appreciate how worthy He is.

WARM-UP

1. What thoughts does the word *worship* bring to your mind? Is the connotation positive or negative? Why?

2. Think about a time when you really felt close to God in worship. What do you think made that time special? If you feel comfortable doing so, share this with the group.

⁶⁶Jesus Himself reemphasized and obeyed the Old Testament command "Worship the Lord your God" (Matthew 4:10). It is the duty (and privilege) of all people to worship their Creator. "Come, let us bow down in worship," says Psalm 95:6, "let us kneel before the Lord our Maker." God clearly expects us to worship. It's our purpose! Godliness without the worship of God is unthinkable. But those who pursue Godliness must realize that it is possible to worship God in vain. Jesus quoted another Old Testament passage to warn of worshiping God vainly: "These people honor me with their lips, but their hearts are far from me. They worship me in vain" (Matthew 15:8-9).

How can we worship God without worshiping in vain? We must learn something that is essential in learning to be like Jesus—the Spiritual Discipline of worship.

Worship Is . . . Focusing on and Responding to God
Worship is difficult to define well. To worship God is to ascribe the proper worth to God, to magnify His worthiness of praise, or better, to approach and address God as He is worthy. He is worthy of all the worth and honor we can give Him and then infinitely more. Notice, for instance, how those around the throne of God in Revelation 4:11 and 5:12 addressed God as "worthy" of so many things.

The more we focus on God, the more we understand and appreciate how worthy He is. As we understand and appreciate this, we can't help but respond to Him. Just as an indescribable sunset or a breathtaking mountaintop vista evokes a spontaneous response, so we cannot encounter the worthiness of God without the response of worship. If you could see God at this moment, you would so utterly understand how worthy He is of worship that you would instinctively fall on your face and worship Him. And to the degree we truly comprehend what God is like, we will respond to Him in worship.

That's why both the public and private worship of God should be based upon and include the Bible, because it reveals God to us so that we may worship Him. Bible reading and preaching are central in public worship because they are the clearest, most direct, most extensive presentation of God in the meeting. For the same reasons, Bible intake and meditation are the heart of private worship.

Worship often includes words and actions, but it goes beyond them to the *focus* of the mind and heart. Worship is the God-centered focus and response of the inner man; it is being preoccupied with God. Since worship is focusing on and responding to God, regardless of what else we are doing we are not worshiping if we are not thinking about God. No matter what you are saying or singing or doing at any moment, you are worshiping God only when you are focused on Him and thinking of Him.

Worship Is ... Done in Spirit and Truth

To worship God in spirit is to worship from the inside out. It means to be sincere in our acts of worship. No matter how spiritual the song you are singing, no matter how poetic the prayer you are praying, if it isn't sincere then it isn't worship, it's hypocrisy.

The balance to worshiping in spirit is to worship in truth. We are to worship according to the truth of Scripture. We worship God as He is revealed in the Bible, not as we might want Him to be.

So we must worship in both spirit and truth, with both heart and head, with both emotions and thought. If we worship too much just by spirit we will be mushy and soft on the truth, worshiping according to feelings. That can lead anywhere from a sleepy tolerance of anything in worship at one extreme to uncontrollable spiritual wildfire on the other. But if we worship by truth without spirit, then our worship will be taut, grim, and icily predictable.

Worship Is ... Expected Both Publicly and Privately

That believers are expected to participate regularly in corporate worship is given in the command of Hebrews 10:25— "Let us not give up meeting together, as some are in the habit of doing."

Christianity is not an isolationist religion. The New Testament describes the Church with metaphors like *body* (1 Corinthians 12:12), *building* (Ephesians 2:21), and *household* (Ephesians 2:19), each of which speaks of the relationship between individual units and a larger whole.

The quality of your private devotional life doesn't exempt you from worshiping with other believers. You may have the devotional life of a George Müller, but you need corporate worship as much as he and the Hebrews did. There's an element of worship and Christianity that cannot be experienced in private worship or by watching worship.

On the other hand, no matter how fulfilling or sufficient our regular public worship celebration seems, there are experiences with God that He gives only in our private worship. Jesus participated faithfully in the public worship of God at the synagogue each Sabbath and at the stated assemblies of Israel at the Temple in Jerusalem. In addition to that, however, Luke observed that "Jesus often withdrew to lonely places and prayed" (5:16). As the familiar Puritan commentator, Matthew Henry, put it, "Public worship will not excuse us from secret worship."[1]

We must not forget that God expects us to worship privately so He can bless us. We minimize our joy when we neglect the daily worship of God in private. Think of it: The Lord Jesus Christ is willing to meet with you privately for as long as you want, and He is willing—even eager—to meet with you every day!

Worship Is ... a Discipline to Be Cultivated
Jesus said, "Worship the Lord your God" (Matthew 4:10). To worship God throughout a lifetime requires discipline. Without discipline, our worship of God will be thin and inconsistent.

True worship is always covered with heartprints. Worship can't be diagramed or calculated, for it is the response of a heart in love with God. And yet, we also must be able to think of worship as a Discipline, a Discipline that must be cultivated just as all relationships must be to remain healthy and grow.

Worship is a Spiritual Discipline insofar as it is both an end and a means. The worship of God is an *end* in itself because worship, as we've defined it, is to focus on and respond to God. There is no higher goal than focusing on and responding to God. But worship is also a *means* in the sense that it is a means to Godliness. The more truly we worship God, the more we become like Him.

People become like their focus. If we would be Godly, we must focus on God. Godliness requires disciplined worship. *(Taken from chapter 5 of* Spiritual Disciplines for the Christian Life.*)*"

Worship Is ... Focusing on and Responding to God

3. Do you agree that "Godliness without the worship of God is unthinkable"? Why, or why not?

4. Describe what it means to "worship God in vain." (See Matthew 15:8-9.)

5. What do the following passages reveal about worship: John 20:28; Revelation 4:8, 5:12-13?

6. According to the following verses, in what ways has God revealed Himself to us so that we might focus on Him?

   John 1:1,14; Hebrews 1:1-2

   Romans 1:20

   2 Timothy 3:16, 2 Peter 1:20-21

Worship Is ... Done in Spirit and Truth

7. What does John 4:23-24 reveal about how God desires His people to worship?

8. What do you think the text means that "to worship God in spirit is to worship from the inside out"?

9. What is the difference between worshiping God as He is revealed in the Bible and worshiping Him as you might want Him to be?

10. One pastor has written, "Where feelings for God are dead, worship is dead."[2] Why is spontaneous affection of the heart so vital to genuine worship?

11. When you don't have the "feelings of worship," does that mean you should stop engaging in forms of worship? Why, or why not?

12. How can we "delight ourselves in the Lord" in our worship? (See Psalm 37:4.)

13. What are the dangers of worshiping just by feelings? Just by truth?

Worship Is . . . Expected Both Publicly and Privately
14. a. What is God's view of corporate worship? (See Hebrews 10:25.)

b. How does this verse conflict with the common assumption that religion is an individual matter only?

15. Consider carefully the comment by Geoffrey Thomas: "There is no way that those who neglect secret worship can know communion with God in the public services of the Lord's day."[3] Do you agree with this statement? Why, or why not?

16. What happens in your life when you neglect the daily worship of God in private?

17. What does Christ's willingness to meet with us privately in worship at any time reveal about His character?

Worship Is . . . a Discipline to Be Cultivated
18. In what ways is it difficult to ask others for help in developing Godliness through public and private worship?

19. Can you identify with the quote: "He worships his work, works at his play, and plays at his worship"? If so, which part(s) do you identify with? Be honest. How might your view of worship be improved?

20. Why do you think it seems easier to worship God one day a week instead of worshiping Him seven days a week? Is one-day-a-week worship even possible? Explain your answer.

CLOSING PRAYER

Focus your mind and heart on the worthiness of God and praise Him for who He is. Thank Him for His willingness to meet with you in worship every day. Focus on His character as revealed in Scripture and respond to Him sincerely. Allow yourself to be fully preoccupied with Him. Allow your deep feelings for Him to well up within you and let them out through praise and adoration.

GOING DEEPER
(Extra questions for further study)

21. What steps can you take this week to improve your private worship? Your public worship?

22. What can you do today to focus more fully on God? On the ways in which He has revealed Himself?

23. Many Christians believe they have "worshiped" if they merely attend church on Sunday. How does what you've learned in this session expand this perspective of worship?

24. The waters of worship should never stop flowing from our hearts, because God is always God and always worthy of worship. If you are not already doing so, how can you channel and distill the flow of your worship into a daily and distinct worship experience?

NOTES
1. John Blanchard, comp., *Gathered Gold* (Welwyn, Hertfordshire, England: Evangelical Press, 1984), page 342.
2. From the book *Desiring God: Meditations of a Christian Hedonist* by John Piper, copyright 1986 by Multnomah Press. Published by Multnomah Press, Portland, Oregon 97266. Used by permission, page 70.
3. Geoffrey Thomas, "Worship in Spirit," *The Banner of Truth*, August–September 1987, page 8.

EVANGELISM...FOR THE PURPOSE OF GODLINESS

CENTRAL IDEA

Evangelism is a natural overflow of the Christian life, but it is also a Discipline. Although all Christians are not expected to use the same *methods* of evangelism, all Christians are expected to evangelize. Godliness requires that we discipline ourselves in the practice of evangelism. The reason many of us don't witness in effective ways is our lack of discipline.

WARM-UP

1. What images does the word *evangelism* bring to mind?

2. Why does God command us to evangelize?

3. Why do you think many Christians are afraid to evangelize? What are your fears about evangelism?

"Only the sheer rapture of being lost in the worship of God is as exhilarating and intoxicating as telling someone about

Jesus Christ. Yet nothing causes an eye-dropping, foot-shuffling anxiety more quickly among a group of Christians like myself than talking about our responsibility to evangelize. In fact, I'm sure I don't know a single Christian who would boldly say, "I am as evangelistic as I should be."

The main idea I want to communicate is that Godliness requires that we discipline ourselves in the practice of evangelism. The reason many of us don't witness for Christ in ways that would be effective and relatively fear-free is simply because we don't discipline ourselves to do it.

Evangelism Is Expected

All Christians are not expected to use the same *methods* of evangelism, but all Christians are expected to evangelize. Before we go further, let's define our terms. What is evangelism? If we want to define it thoroughly, we could say that evangelism is to present Jesus Christ in the power of the Holy Spirit to sinful people, in order that they may come to put their trust in God through Him, to receive Him as their Savior, and serve Him as their King in the fellowship of His Church.[1] If we want to define it simply, we could say that New Testament evangelism is communicating the gospel. Anyone who faithfully relates the essential elements of God's salvation through Jesus Christ is evangelizing. This is true whether your words are spoken, written, or recorded, and whether they are delivered to one person or to a crowd.

Why is evangelism expected? The Lord Jesus Christ Himself has commanded us to witness. Consider His authority in the following: "Therefore go and make disciples of all nations, baptizing them in the name of the Father and of the Son and of the Holy Spirit, and teaching them to obey everything I have commanded you. And surely I will be with you always, to the very end of the age" (Matthew 28:19-20). Again Jesus said, "Peace be with you! As the Father has sent me, I am sending you" (John 20:21).

These commands weren't given to the apostles only. For example, the apostles never came to *this* nation, and the apostles will never come to your home, your neighborhood, or to the place where you work. For the Great Commission to be fulfilled, for Christ to have a witness in that "remote part" of the earth, a Christian like you must discipline yourself to do it.

Evangelism Is Empowered

If it is so obvious to almost all Christians that we are to evangelize, how come almost all Christians seem to disobey that command so often? Some believe that they need a lot of specialized training to witness effectively. They are afraid to talk to someone about Christ until they feel confident that they have an adequate amount of Bible knowledge and could deal with any potential question or objection.

The problem is that confident day never comes. Sometimes we are unable to speak of Christ because we are afraid that people will think we are strange and will reject us. In some cases the method of witnessing we're asked to use causes our evangelophobia. If it requires approaching someone we've never met before and striking up a conversation about Christ, most people will be terrified and indicate it by their absence. I think the seriousness of evangelism is the main reason it frightens us. We realize that in talking with someone about Christ, Heaven and hell are at stake. The eternal destiny of the person is the issue. Many Christians feel too unprepared for this kind of challenge.

What is success in evangelism? Is it when the person you witness to comes to Christ? Certainly that's what we want to happen. But if this is success, are we failures whenever we share the gospel and people refuse to believe? Was Jesus an "evangelistic failure" when people like the rich young ruler turned away from Him and His message? Obviously not.

We need to learn that sharing the gospel *is* successful evangelism. We ought to have an obsession for souls and tearfully plead with God to see more people converted, but conversions are fruit that God alone can give. In this regard we are like the postal service. Success is measured by the careful and accurate delivery of the message, not by the response of the recipient. Whenever we share the gospel (which includes the summons to repent and believe), we have succeeded. In the truest sense, *all* biblical evangelism is successful evangelism, regardless of the results.

The power of evangelism is the Holy Spirit. From the instant that He indwells us He gives us the power to witness. Jesus stressed this in Acts 1:8. We are not all empowered to evangelize the same way, but all believers have been given power to be witnesses of Jesus Christ. The evidence that you've been given the power to witness is a changed life. The

51

same Holy Spirit power that changed your life for Christ is the power to witness for Christ. So if God by His Spirit has changed your life, be confident of this: God has given you Acts 1:8 power, and the Holy Spirit may grant much power to your witness in an evangelistic encounter without giving to you any *feeling* or *sense* of power in it.

We can be confident that some will believe if we will faithfully and tenaciously share the gospel. It is the *gospel* that is the power of God for salvation and not our own eloquent power or persuasiveness. God has His elect whom He will call and whom He has chosen to call *through the gospel* (Romans 8:29-30, 10:17).

There is also a power for evangelism in the one living a sincere Christian life. Paul describes the power of Godliness in 2 Corinthians 2:14-17, which says that the Lord empowers the life and the words of the faithful believer with a power of spiritual attraction. The most powerful ongoing Christian witness has always been the speaking of God's Word by one who is living God's Word.

Evangelism Is a Discipline

Evangelism is a natural overflow of the Christian life. We should all be able to talk about what the Lord has done for us and what He means to us. But evangelism is also a *Discipline* in that we must discipline ourselves to get into the context of evangelism, not just wait for witnessing opportunities to happen.

Jesus said in Matthew 5:16, "Let your light shine before men, that they may see your good deeds and praise your Father in heaven." Any Christian who has heard biblical preaching, participated in Bible studies, and read the Scriptures and Christian literature for any time at all should have enough understanding of the basic message of Christianity to share it with someone else. Even so, many Christians don't actively witness.

Isn't the reason we don't witness because we don't *discipline* ourselves to do it? Yes, there are those wonderful, unplanned opportunities "to give the reason for the hope that you have" (1 Peter 3:15) that God brings unexpectedly. But most Christians haven't disciplined themselves to act on these opportunities. So, the point is not how many unbelievers you see every day, but how often you are with them in an appropriate context for sharing the gospel. Despite the important work-related conversations you may have throughout the day, how often do you have meaningful conversations with coworkers where spiritual issues can be raised?

That's why I say evangelism is a Spiritual Discipline. Unless we discipline ourselves for evangelism, it is very easy to excuse ourselves from ever sharing the gospel with anyone. You'll have to discipline yourself to ask your neighbors how you can pray for them or when you can share a meal with them. You'll have to discipline yourself to get with your coworkers during off-hours. Many such opportunities for evangelism will never take place if you wait for them to occur spontaneously. The world, the flesh, and the Devil will do their best to see to that. You, however, backed by the invincible power of the Holy Spirit, can make sure that these enemies of the gospel do not win.

Regardless of how shy or unskilled we may feel about evangelism, we must not convince ourselves that we cannot or will not verbally share the gospel. Often it is the message of the Cross *lived and demonstrated* that God uses to open a heart to the gospel, but it is the message of the Cross *proclaimed* (by word or page) through which the power of God saves those who believe its content. No matter how well we live the gospel (and we must live it well, else we hinder its reception), sooner or later we must communicate the *content* of the gospel before a person can become a disciple of Jesus. *(Taken from chapter 6 of* Spiritual Disciplines for the Christian Life.*)*❞

Evangelism Is Expected
4. According to Acts 1:8, in whose power are we to witness (as opposed to doing it in our own power)?

5. What do the following verses reveal about evangelism?

Luke 24:27

John 20:21

53

6. Why do you think God commands all of His people to evangelize and not just those who find it easy to present themselves and their beliefs to other people?

7. What does 1 Peter 2:9 say about God's people?

Evangelism Is Empowered

8. We read in John 9 about the blind man Jesus healed. What is striking about his words to the Pharisees?

9. According to this John 9 passage, when should we witness?

10. Have you ever been afraid to share Christ? If so, when? Why were you afraid?

11. With which evangelistic approach(es) are you most comfortable? Which ones intimidate you? Be honest.

12. Discuss with your group the kinds of responses—positive and negative—you received when you shared the good news of Christ with others.

13. Researcher George Barna says that most Christians who witness to others come away feeling like failures. So, since they don't like to fail, they redirect their efforts into spiritual activities in which they are more likely to be satisfied and successful. Have you found this to be true? Why, or why not?

14. Are you confident that God has given you Acts 1:8 power? Why, or why not?

15. What does 2 Corinthians 2:14-17 say about God's power through us? About our impact on nonChristians?

16. What does Colossians 4:5-6 say about how to approach evangelism? Why is such preparation so important?

17. Consider ways you might begin to make evangelism a Spiritual Discipline. What steps can you take this week to build deeper relationships with unbelievers?

18. It is said that every Christian is at every moment a testimony—good or bad—to the power of Jesus Christ. What implications does this truth have in evangelism?

CLOSING PRAYER

Focus on what God has done for you and on the importance of sharing Him with others. Ask the Lord to nurture the Discipline of evangelism this week. Ask Him to guide you to at least one person who is hungry for His truths.

GOING DEEPER
(Extra questions for further study)

19. Why is it necessary to communicate the gospel's content in addition to living out its truths daily?

20. Which excuses have you used in order to avoid evangelizing your friends? Neighbors? Coworkers? Family members?

21. Write down the names of two people with whom you want to share Christ soon, perhaps even this week. What loving, sensitive steps are you willing to take in order to seek ways of intentionally sharing Christ with them? A lunch meeting? A home meeting? Other?

22. Part of becoming more Christlike is to seek forgiveness for and to eliminate the sin in our lives that makes our words and actions seem inconsistent with our faith. Which sins in your life are creating an obstacle in your willingness and ability to witness?

23. Do you agree that "the more Christlike our lives are, the more convincing our words about Christ will be"? Answer using an illustration from your life.

NOTE
1. See J. I. Packer, *Evangelism and the Sovereignty of God* (Downers Grove, IL: InterVarsity Press, 1979), pages 37-57.

SERVING...FOR THE PURPOSE OF GODLINESS

CENTRAL IDEA

To serve the Lord with gladness is every Christian's commission. In God's Kingdom, no one is spiritually unemployed or retired. Everyone is gifted to serve, with the goal of being more like Jesus. If we don't discipline ourselves to serve for the sake of Christ and His Kingdom, we'll serve only occasionally or when it's convenient or self-serving. The result will be a quantity and quality of service that we'll regret when the Day of Accountability for our service comes.

WARM-UP

1. What, in your mind, is a *servant*? Describe the feelings you have about being a servant of Christ and His Kingdom. Be honest!

2. Would you agree that most servers receive little appreciation for their efforts? If so, why is this? If not, what type of recognition do they receive?

3. If Jesus were to come back to earth today, what types of ministry service would you wish you had done?

❝Serving God is not a job for the casually interested. It's costly service. He asks for your life. He asks for service to Him to become a priority, not a pastime.

The ministry of serving may be as public as preaching or teaching, but more often it will be as sequestered as nursery duty. Serving may be as appreciated as a good testimony in a worship service, but typically it's as thankless as washing dishes after a church social. Most service, even that which seems the most glamorous, is like an iceberg. Only the eye of God ever sees the larger, hidden part of it.

Serving is as commonplace as the practical needs it seeks to meet. That's why serving must become a Spiritual Discipline. The flesh connives against its hiddenness and sameness. Two of the deadliest of our sins—sloth and pride—loathe serving. So if we don't discipline ourselves to serve for the sake of Christ and His Kingdom (and for the purpose of Godliness), we'll "serve" only occasionally or when it's con-venient or *self*-serving. The result will be a quantity and qual-ity of service we'll regret when the Day of Accountability for our service comes.

Every Christian Is Expected to Serve
When we are born again and our sins are forgiven, the blood of Christ cleanses our conscience, according to Hebrews 9:14, in order for us to "serve the living God!" "Serve the LORD with gladness" (Psalm 100:2, NASB) is every Christian's com-mission. There is no such thing as spiritual unemployment or spiritual retirement in the Kingdom of God. Of course, motives matter in the service we are to offer to God. The Bible mentions at least six motives for serving.

Motivated by obedience. In Deuteronomy 13:4, Moses wrote, "It is the Lord your God you must follow, and him you must revere. Keep his commands and obey him; serve him and hold fast to him." Everything in that verse relates to obe-dience to God. We should serve the Lord because we want to obey Him.

How can any professing Christian think it is okay to sit on the spiritual sidelines and watch others do the work of the

Kingdom? Any true Christian would say that he or she wants to obey God. But we disobey God when we are not serving Him. Not to serve God is sinful.

Motivated by gratitude. The prophet Samuel exhorted the people of God to service with these words: "Be sure to fear the LORD and serve Him faithfully with all your heart; consider what great things he has done for you" (1 Samuel 12:24). It is no burden to serve God when we consider what great things He has done for us. He has never done anything greater for anyone, nor could He do anything greater for you, than bring you to Himself. If we cannot be grateful servants of Him who is everything and in whom we have everything, what *will* make us grateful?

Motivated by gladness. The inspired command of Psalm 100:2 is, "Serve the LORD with gladness" (NASB). We are not to serve God grudgingly or grimly, but gladly.

For the believer, serving God is not a burden, it's a privilege. I can understand why the person who serves God in an attempt to earn his way to Heaven doesn't serve with gladness. But the Christian who gratefully acknowledges what God has done for him for eternity should be able to serve God cheerfully and with joy.

Motivated by forgiveness, not guilt. In Isaiah's famous vision of God, he became eager to serve the Lord once his sins were forgiven (Isaiah 6:6-8). Like a dog on a leash, Isaiah was straining out of his skin to serve God in some way, *any* way. Because he felt guilty? No! Because God had taken his guilt *away!*

The people of God do not serve Him in order *to be* forgiven but *because we are* forgiven. When believers serve only because they feel guilty if they don't, it's as though they serve with a ball and chain dragging from their ankles. There's no love in that kind of service, only labor. There's no joy, only obligation and drudgery. But Christians aren't prisoners who should serve in God's Kingdom grudgingly because of guilt. We can serve willingly because Christ's death freed us from guilt.

Motivated by humility. Jesus was the perfect Servant. With astonishing humility, Jesus washed the feet of His disciples as an example of how all His followers should serve with humility.

In this life a part of us (the Bible calls it the *flesh*) will

always say, "If I have to serve, I want to get something for it."
But this isn't Christlike service. This is hypocrisy. By the
power of the Holy Spirit we must reject self-righteous service
as a sinful motivation, and serve "in humility," considering
"others better" than ourselves (Philippians 2:3).

Motivated by love. At the heart of service, according to
Galatians 5:13, should be love: "You, my brothers, were
called to be free. But do not use your freedom to indulge the
sinful nature; rather, serve one another in love." There is no
better fuel for service that burns longer and provides more
energy than love.

Jesus said in Mark 12:28-31 that the greatest command is
to love God with all you are, and the next most important one
is to love your neighbor as you love yourself. In light of these
words, surely the more we love God the more we will live for
Him and serve Him, and the more we love others the more we
will serve them.

Every Christian Is Gifted to Serve
At the moment of salvation when the Holy Spirit comes to
live within you, He brings a gift with Him. We're told in
1 Corinthians 12:4,11 that there are many different varieties
of gifts, and the Holy Spirit determines by His sovereign will
which gift goes to which believer. Even more specific is
1 Peter 4:10, which certifies that each Christian is specially
gifted and that the purpose for that gift is service.

If this is among the first times you have heard about spiritual gifts, then you probably have no idea what your gift is.
Relax. Many Christians serve God faithfully and fruitfully for
a lifetime without ascertaining their specific gift. I'm not sug-
gesting you shouldn't try to identify your gift; I'm saying that
you aren't relegated to bench-warmer status in the Kingdom
of God until you can name your gift

By all means, don't be discouraged from serving. I
encourage you to discipline yourself to serve in a regular,
ongoing ministry in your local church. It doesn't necessarily
have to be in a recognized or elected position. But find a way
to defeat the temptation to serve only when it's convenient or
exciting. That's not disciplined service.

Serving Is Often Hard Work
Some teach that once you discover and employ your spiritual
gift, then serving becomes nothing but effortless joy. But

that's not New Testament Christianity. The Apostle Paul wrote in Ephesians 4:12 of "the equipping of the saints for the *work* of service" (NASB, emphasis mine). Sometimes serving God and others is nothing less than hard work. Paul describes his service to God with these words in Colossians 1:29—"To this end I labor, struggling with all his energy, which so powerfully works in me." The word *labor* means to work to the point of exhaustion, while from the Greek word translated "struggling" comes our word *agonize*.

God supplies us with the power to serve Him. We struggle in service "with all his energy, which so powerfully works" in us. True ministry is never forced out by the flesh. But the result of his power working mightily in us is "labor." That means when you serve the Lord in a local church or in any type of ministry, it will often be hard. If you are like Paul, sometimes it will be agonizing and exhausting. It will take time. There will always be more entertaining things you could be doing. And if for no other reason, serving God is hard work because it means serving people. But remember that service costing nothing accomplishes nothing.

Serving God is work, but there's no work so rewarding or enduring.

Are you willing to serve? The Israelites knew without a doubt that God *expected* them to serve Him, but Joshua once looked them in the eye and challenged them on their *willingness* to serve: "If serving the LORD seems undesirable to you, then choose for yourselves this day whom you will serve. . . . But as for me and my household, we will serve the LORD" (Joshua 24:15).

The Lord Jesus was always the servant, the servant of all, the servant of servants, *the Servant*. He said, "I am among you as the one who serves" (Luke 22:27). If we are to be like Christ, we must discipline ourselves to serve as Jesus served. *(Taken from chapter 7 of* Spiritual Disciplines for the Christian Life.*)*"

Every Christian Is Expected to Serve
4. Why, according to Hebrews 9:14, does the blood of Christ cleanse our conscience when we become Christians?

5. What does it mean to "serve the LORD with gladness" (Psalm 100:2)?

6. What does Psalm 84:10 show us about David's view of service?

7. Why should we serve the Lord? (Deuteronomy 13:4)

8. The text states, "It is no burden to serve God when we consider what great things He has done for us." What great things has God done for you? Be specific.

9. Read Isaiah 6:6-8. What was Isaiah's response to God? Why?

10. C. H. Spurgeon said in a sermon in 1867, "The child of God works not *for* life but *from* life; he does not work *to be* saved, he works *because* he is saved."[1] Describe in your own words what he is saying.

11. What can we learn about humble service from each of these passages?

Mark 12:28-31

John 13:12-16

Philippians 2:3

12. Why is it so easy for us to serve people for the wrong reasons? If you feel free to do so, share a time when you served for the wrong reasons.

13. What, according to Galatians 5:13, is at the heart of disciplined service?

Every Christian Is Gifted to Serve
14. What do each of the following passages reveal about spiritual gifts: 1 Corinthians 12:4-11,27-31; Ephesians 4:7-13; 1 Peter 4:10-11?

15. What do you consider your gift to be? (Read Romans 12:4-8.) Why?

16. How does Colossians 1:29 apply to the work God may be calling you to do?

17. Do you agree that "service costing nothing accomplishes nothing"? Explain your answer.

18. What does Jesus call the satisfying work of serving God? (See John 4:34.)

19. a. What promise does God make concerning our service to Him?

    1 Corinthians 15:58

    Hebrews 5:10

    b. Does that mean we'll always see the fruit of our labors? Why, or why not?

CLOSING PRAYER

Review the six motives for serving mentioned in this chapter. Then express to God the following. Be honest with Him and ask Him to help you grow in these areas:

- Your desire to obey Him.
- Your gratitude for what He has done for you.
- Your willingness to serve Him gladly.
- Your joy at being forgiven.
- Your desire to learn humility.
- Your love for Him and desire to love others.

GOING DEEPER
(Extra questions for further study)

20. What can you do to make service for God a greater priority in your daily life?

21. What is the difference between serving someone as an act of love and righteousness and serving someone in order to train yourself away from covetousness, arrogance, envy, possessiveness, or resentment?

22. It's said that "worship empowers serving; serving expresses worship." What is the relationship between service, on the one hand, and regular personal and corporate worship? Why are both so intertwined?

NOTE
1. C. H. Spurgeon, "Serving the Lord with Gladness," in *Metropolitan Tabernacle Pulpit* (London: Passmore and Alabaster, 1868; reprint, Pasadena, TX: Pilgrim Publications, 1989), vol. 13, pages 495-496.

STEWARDSHIP...FOR THE PURPOSE OF GODLINESS

CENTRAL IDEA

The clock and the dollar greatly influence our lives, so we must consider their role in Godly living. God calls us to be disciplined in the use of our time and our money. Godliness is the result of a disciplined spiritual life, but the Discipline of time and the Discipline of money are at the heart of a disciplined spiritual life that leads to Christlikeness.

WARM-UP

1. Why do you think people have difficulty managing their money? Which cultural and personal factors contribute to this difficulty?

2. Do you often feel that "there aren't enough hours in the day"? What are some of the reasons why people feel so much time pressure?

3. When someone mentions your need to be a better steward of money and time, how do you typically respond?

The Disciplined Use of Time

❝Godliness is the result of a disciplined spiritual life. But at the heart of a disciplined spiritual life is the Discipline of time. If we are going to be like Jesus, we must see the use of our time as a Spiritual Discipline. Having so perfectly ordered His moments and His days, at the end of His earthly life Jesus was able to pray to the Father, "I have brought you glory on earth by completing the work you gave me to do" (John 17:4). Here are ten biblical reasons for the disciplined use of time (many of which were made clear to me in the reading of Jonathan Edwards' sermon on "The Preciousness of Time and the Importance of Redeeming It").

Use time wisely "because the days are evil." To use time wisely "because the days are evil" is a curious phrase embedded in the inspired language of the Apostle Paul in Ephesians 5:15-16. The days are evil still. Even without the kind of persecution or opposition known by the Christians of Paul's day, the world we live in is not conducive to using time wisely, especially for purposes of spirituality and Godliness.

The natural course of our minds, our bodies, our world, and our days leads us toward evil, not toward Christlikeness. *Thoughts* must be disciplined, otherwise, like water, they tend to flow downhill or stand stagnant. Our *bodies* are inclined to ease, pleasure, gluttony, and sloth. Unless we practice self-control, our bodies will tend to serve evil more than God. Finally, our *days* are days of active evil because every temptation and evil force is active in them.

Wise use of time is the preparation for eternity. You must prepare for eternity in time. During time (that is, in this life) you must prepare for eternity, for there will be no second chance to prepare once you have crossed eternity's timeless threshold. We must prepare for eternity *in time*—that is, prepare before it is too late.

What is more precious than time? For as a small rudder determines the direction of a great ocean liner, so that which is done in time influences eternity. Come to God in time, and He will bring you to Himself in eternity.

Time is short. Time would not be so precious if we never died. But since we are never more than a breath away from eternity, the way we use our time has eternal significance. But even if you have decades of life remaining, the fact is, "You are a mist that appears for a little while and then vanishes" (James 4:14). Even the longest life is brief in comparison to eternity.

Time is passing. Not only is time short, but what does remain is fleeting. The rest of your life is not like a small block of ice you can take from the freezer and use when you are ready. Instead, time is very much like the sands in an hourglass—what's left is slipping by. If you don't discipline your use of time for the purpose of Godliness now, it won't be any easier later.

The remaining time is uncertain. Not only is time short and passing, but we do not even know how short it actually is or how quickly it will pass. That's why the wisdom of Proverbs 27:1 is, "Do not boast about tomorrow, for you do not know what a day may bring forth." Obviously, we must make certain kinds of plans as though we were going to live for many more years. But there is a very real sense in which we must use our time for the purpose of Godliness as though it were uncertain that we would live tomorrow, for that is a very certain uncertainty.

Time lost cannot be regained. Once it is gone, it is gone forever. God has offered you this time to discipline yourself for the purpose of Godliness. Jesus said in John 9:4, "As long as it is day, we must do the work of him who sent me. Night is coming, when no one can work." The time for the works of God, that is, Godly living, is now, while it is "day."

You are accountable to God for your time. There's hardly a more sobering statement in Scripture than Romans 14:12— "So then, each one of us will give an account of himself to God." The words "each one of us" apply to Christians and nonChristians alike. And though believers will be saved by grace and not by works, once in Heaven our reward will be determined on the basis of our works. The wise response to such truth is to evaluate your use of time now and spend it in a way that you would like to hear at the Judgment. And if you cannot answer your conscience regarding how you use your time in the growth of Christlikeness now, how will you be able to answer God then?

Time is so easily lost. Except for the "fool," no other character in the book of Proverbs draws the scorn of Scripture like the slothful "sluggard." The reason? His lazy and wasteful use of time.

Time appears to be so plentiful that losing much of it seems inconsequential. Yet time is infinitely more precious than money because money can't buy time. But you can minimize the loss and waste of time by disciplining yourself for the purpose of Godliness.

We value time at death. As the one who is out of money values it most when it is gone, so do we at death value time most when it is gone. If additional years were given to us at death, it would profit nothing unless we made a change in how we used our time. So the time to value time is now, and not just at death.

Time's value in eternity. If there are any regrets in Heaven, they will only be that we did not use our earthly time more for the glory of God and for growth in His grace. If this is so, this may be Heaven's only similarity with hell, which will be filled with agonizing laments over time so foolishly squandered. In Luke 16:25, the Bible portrays this anguish over a wasted lifetime in the story of the rich man who went to Hades and of Lazarus who went to "Abraham's bosom." If those in the merciless side of eternity owned a thousand worlds, they would give them all (if they could) for one of our days.

The Disciplined Use of Money

The Bible relates not only the use of time to our spiritual condition, but also our use of money. Why is a biblical use of our money and resources so crucial to our growth in Godliness? For one thing it's a matter of sheer obedience. A surprisingly large amount of Scripture deals with the use of wealth and possessions. If we ignore it or take it lightly, our "Godliness" will be a sham. But as much as anything else, the reason the use of money and the things it buys is one of the best indicators of spiritual maturity and Godliness is that we exchange such a great part of our lives for it. Because we invest most of our days working in exchange for money, there is a very real sense in which our money represents *us*. Therefore, how we use it expresses who we are, what our priorities are, and what's in our hearts. Growth in Godliness will express itself in a growing understanding of these New Testament principles of giving.

God owns everything you own. In 1 Corinthians 10:26, the Apostle Paul quotes Psalm 24:1, which reads, "The earth is the LORD's, and everything in it." God owns everything, including everything you possess, because He created everything. God wants us to use and enjoy the things He has allowed us to have, but as stewards of them we're to remember that they belong to Him and they are primarily to be used for His Kingdom. So the question is not, "How much of my money should I give to God?" but rather, "How much of God's money should I keep for myself?"

Giving is an act of worship. In Philippians 4:18, the Apostle Paul thanks the Christians in the Grecian city of Philippi for the financial gift they gave in support of his missionary ministry. He calls the money they gave "a fragrant offering, an acceptable sacrifice, pleasing to God," comparing it to an Old Testament sacrifice people gave in worship to God. In other words, Paul says that their act of giving to the work of God was an act of worshiping God. Giving is much more than a duty or an obligation, it is an act of worshiping the Lord.

Giving reflects faith in God's provision. The proportion of your income that you give back to God is one distinct indication of how much you trust Him to provide for your needs. We will give to the extent that we believe God will provide for us. The more we believe God will provide for our needs, the more we are willing to risk giving to Him. And the less we trust God, the less we will give to Him.

Giving should be sacrificial and generous. Giving isn't sacrificial unless it's a sacrifice. Many professing Christians give only token amounts to the work of God's Kingdom. A much smaller number give well, while perhaps only a few actually give sacrificially. A Gallup Poll from October 1988 shows that the more money Americans make, the *less* sacrificial our giving becomes.

I've never known anyone who gave sacrificially—whether through a one-time sacrificial gift or consistent sacrificial offerings—who regretted it. Sure, they missed having some things they could have had if they'd spent the money on themselves. But the joy and fulfillment they gained by giving away something they could not ultimately keep was

70

more than worth it.

Giving reflects spiritual trustworthiness. This is a startling insight into the ways of God's Kingdom that Jesus reveals to us in Luke 16:10-13. If we are not faithful with the use of our money, and certainly that includes the giving of our money for Christ's Kingdom, the Bible says God will determine that we are untrustworthy to handle spiritual riches.

The use of your money and how you give it is one of the best ways of evaluating your relationship with Christ and your spiritual trustworthiness. If you love Christ with all your heart, your giving will reflect that. That's why it's said that your checkbook tells more about you than almost anything else.

Giving—love, not legalism. God does not send you a bill. The church does not send you a bill. Giving to God and to the support of the work of His Kingdom isn't done in fulfillment of some "eleventh commandment." Your giving should be motivated by your love for God. How much you give should be a reflection of how much you love God. He wants your giving to be an expression of your love for Him, not of legalism.

Give willingly, thankfully, and cheerfully. "Each man should give what he has decided in his heart to give, not reluctantly or under compulsion, for God loves a cheerful giver" (2 Corinthians 9:7). God doesn't want you to give with a grudge—that is, you give but you don't want to—resentfully, with a heart that isn't right no matter how much you give. He wants you to give because you want to. When you think of how God has given you the greatest possible gift in His Son, Jesus Christ, when you think of the mercy and grace He has given you, when you think of how He has provided all you have, and when you think that you're giving to *God*, you should be able to give thankfully and cheerfully.

Giving should be planned and systematic. Notice how the Apostle Paul directs the Christians to give in 1 Corinthians 16:1-2—"Now about the collection for God's people: Do what I told the Galatian churches to do. On the first day of every week, each one of you should set aside a sum of money in keeping with his income, saving it up, so that when I come no collections will have to be made."

Notice three things about this planned, systematic giving. He told them to give "on the first day of every week."

Second, note that he says "each of you should" do this. All who claim to be believers are to express their stewardship of God's money this way. Third, he says that each is to give "in keeping with his income," or "as he may prosper" (NASB). The more you prosper, the higher should be the proportion of your giving.

Generous giving results in bountiful blessing. Our Lord Jesus said in Luke 6:38, "Give, and it will be given to you. A good measure, pressed down, shaken together and running over, will be poured into your lap. For with the measure you use, it will be measured to you."

God never says that if you give faithfully He will give you a lot of money, or some other specific earthly blessing. But He does say He will bless you in this life if you love Him enough and trust Him enough to be generous in your giving to Him. *(Taken from chapter 8 of* Spiritual Disciplines for the Christian Life.)**

The Disciplined Use of Time

4. Reread John 17:4. What work do you believe God has given you to do? How well are you completing it?

5. According to Ephesians 5:15-16, "the days are evil." Why, therefore, are we to make the most of our time? How do we do this?

6. Which things hinder you from using your time the way God would have you use it? Be honest.

7. What must you do to obey the command found in Colossians 3:2?

8. How strongly do you believe in the existence of evil spirits today? In what ways does a person's view of evil influence the time he or she spends in the Christian Disciplines?

9. Read 2 Corinthians 6:2 and James 4:14. If you knew you'd be in eternity tomorrow, how would you live life differently today?

10. What circumstances have reminded you that time is passing and death might be near? (See Psalm 31:15.)

11. a. Consider ways in which you've misused time. If you feel comfortable doing so, share them with the group. Also state your most effective means of minimizing the misuse of time.

   b. Read Philippians 3:13-14. What is the will of God for us, despite the ways in which we've misused time?

12. What does Hebrews 5:12 say about using our time to gain spiritual maturity?

13. Look up Matthew 12:36, 25:14-30. What do they say about God's judgment of our actions?

14. What does Proverbs 5:11-13, 24:33-34 say about lost time and opportunity?

The Disciplined Use of Money

15. Is it easy to grasp that God owns everything we possess? Why, or why not?

16. a. What does Luke 16:10-13 say about who God can trust?

    b. Why do you think Luke likens money to a "master"?

17. In what ways can you excel in love by giving? (See 2 Corinthians 8:7.)

18. Why should you give to God willingly, thankfully, and cheerfully?

19. If you are meeting in a group, discuss the meaning of each phrase in 2 Corinthians 9:6-8.

CLOSING PRAYER
Thank God for His love, faithfulness, provision, and—most important of all—for giving His Son as a sacrifice for your sins. Ask Him to reveal ways in which you can better use time and money for the purpose of Godliness.

GOING DEEPER
(Extra questions for further study)
20. What are the benefits of a systematic giving plan?

21. What specific steps are you willing to take to implement needed changes in your giving?

22. Are you preparing, through your stewardship of time and money, to stand before God and give an account of your use of time and money? Explain your answer.

23. In light of many people's burnout-prone lifestyle, what can you learn from Ecclesiastes 3:1? In which areas of your life are you too rushed and becoming emotionally and physically drained?

FASTING, SILENCE, AND SOLITUDE...FOR THE PURPOSE OF GODLINESS

CENTRAL IDEA
Many of us do not know much about the Discipline of fasting, so we tend to misunderstand and fear it. It's also hard for us to so radically go against the mainstream of culture by fasting. Yet purposeful fasting provides strong benefits in the disciplined pursuit of a Christlike life. It is a discipline that Jesus both taught and practiced. Likewise, the Disciplines of silence and solitude, which Jesus diligently practiced, are foreign to many who have learned to be comfortable only with noise and crowds. Yet these Disciplines contribute much to our spiritual growth and development.

WARM-UP
1. Describe what you think fasting means. Include what you consider to be positive and negative aspects of fasting.

2. Describe what you have learned about fasting from other Christians.

3. Have you ever chosen to temporarily seek privacy for spiritual purposes? If so, describe what it was like.

FASTING . . . FOR THE PURPOSE OF GODLINESS
❝Christians in a gluttonous, denial-less, self-indulgent society may struggle to accept and to begin the practice of fasting. Few Disciplines go so radically against the flesh and the mainstream of culture as this one. But we cannot overlook its biblical significance. Of course, some people, for medical reasons, cannot fast. But most of us dare not overlook fasting's benefits in the disciplined pursuit of a Christlike life.

Fasting Explained
A biblical definition of fasting is a Christian's voluntary abstinence from food for spiritual purposes. It is *Christian*, for fasting by a nonChristian obtains no eternal value because the Discipline's motives and purposes are to be God-centered. It is *voluntary* in that fasting is not to be coerced. Fasting is more than just the ultimate crash diet for the body; it is abstinence from food for *spiritual* purposes.

The Bible distinguishes between several kinds of fasts.

- A *normal fast* involves abstaining from all food, but not from water.
- A *partial fast* is a limitation of the diet but not abstention from all food.
- An *absolute fast* is the avoidance of all food and liquid, even water.
- The Bible also describes a *supernatural* fast that requires God's supernatural intervention into the bodily processes.
- A *private fast* is what Jesus was speaking of in Matthew 6:16-18 when He says we should fast in a way not to be noticed by others.
- *Congregational fasts* are the type found in Joel 2:15-16 and Acts 13:2.
- The Bible also speaks of *national fasts*. See 2 Chronicles 20:3, Nehemiah 9:1, Esther 4:16, and Jonah 3:5-8.
- There was one *regular fast* that God commanded under

77

the Old Covenant. Every Jew was to fast on the Day of Atonement (Leviticus 16:29-31).

- Finally, the Bible mentions *occasional fasts.* These occur on special occasions as the need arises.

Fasting Is Expected

Notice Jesus' words at the beginning of Matthew 6:16-17— "And *when* you fast. . . . But *when* you fast. . . ." By giving us instructions on what to do and what not to do when we fast, Jesus assumes that we will fast. Plainer still are His words in Matthew 9:14-15—Jesus said that the time would come when His disciples "will fast," and that time is now.

Until Jesus, the Bridegroom of the Church, returns, He expects us to fast. Yet He gives us no command regarding how often or how long we should fast. Just like all other Spiritual Disciplines, fasting is not to be a legalistic routine. It is a privilege and an opportunity to seek God's grace.

Fasting Is to Be Done for a Purpose

Without a purpose, fasting can be a miserable, self-centered experience. Many purposes for fasting are given in Scripture. I've condensed them into ten major categories. Whenever you fast, you should do so for at least one of these purposes. (Notice that *none* of the purposes is to earn God's favor, to impress Him and earn His acceptance. We are made acceptable to God through the work of Christ Jesus, not our work.)

To strengthen prayer. There's something about fasting that sharpens the edge of our intercessions and gives passion to our supplications. So it has frequently been used by the people of God when there is a special urgency about the concerns they lift before the Father. The Bible does not teach that fasting is a kind of spiritual hunger strike that compels God to do our bidding. If we ask for something outside of God's will, fasting does not cause Him to reconsider. Fasting does not change God's hearing so much as it changes our praying.

To seek God's guidance. There is biblical precedent for fasting for the purpose of more clearly discerning the will of God. Fasting does not *ensure* the certainty of receiving clear guidance from God. Rightly practiced, however, it does make us more receptive to the One who loves to guide us.

To express grief. As mentioned in Judges 20:26, the

Israelites wept and fasted to express grief for the forty thousand brothers they had lost in battle. Grief caused by events other than a death can also be expressed through fasting. Christians have fasted because of grief for their sins and as a means of expressing grief for sins of others.

To seek deliverance or protection. One of the most common fasts in biblical times was a fast to seek salvation from enemies or circumstances. Fasting, rather than fleshly efforts, should be one of our first defenses against persecution because of our faith.

To express repentance and the return to God. Fasting for this purpose is similar to fasting for the purpose of expressing grief for sin. But as repentance is a change of mind resulting in a change of action, fasting can represent more than just grief over sin. It can signal a commitment to obedience and a new direction.

To humble oneself before God. Fasting, when practiced with the right motives, is a physical expression of humility before God, just as kneeling or prostrating yourself in prayer can reflect humility before Him.

To express concern for the work of God. Just as a parent might fast and pray out of concern for the work of God in the life of a child, so Christians may fast and pray because they feel a burden for the work of God in a broader scope. A Christian might feel compelled to fast and pray for the work of God in a place that has experienced tragedy, disappointment, or apparent defeat.

To minister to the needs of others. Those who think the Spiritual Disciplines foster tendencies of introspection or independence should consider Isaiah 58:6-7. In the most extensive passage in Scripture dealing exclusively with fasting, God emphasizes fasting for the purpose of meeting the needs of others.

To overcome temptation and dedicate yourself to God. Ask Christians to name a fast by a biblical character and most will probably think first of the supernatural fast of Jesus prior to His temptation in Matthew 4:1-11. There are times we struggle with temptation, or we *anticipate* grappling with it, when we need extra spiritual strength to overcome it. Fasting for the purpose of overcoming the temptation and of renewing our dedication to God is a Christlike response.

To express love and worship to God. Fasting can be an

expression of finding your greatest pleasure and enjoyment in life from God. That's the case when disciplining yourself to fast means that you love God more than food, that seeking Him is more important to you than eating. This honors God and is a means of worshiping Him as God.

There is no doubt that God has often crowned fasting with extraordinary blessings, but we should be careful not to have what Martyn Lloyd-Jones called a mechanical view of fasting. We cannot manipulate God to do our bidding by fasting any more than we can by any other means. As with prayer, we fast in hope that by His *grace* God *will* bless us as we desire. God will bless a rightly motivated, biblical fast by any of His children. Whether or not you receive the blessing you hope for, one thing is sure: If you knew what God knew, you would give yourself the identical blessing that He does. And none of His rewards is worthless. *(Taken from chapter 9 of* Spiritual Disciplines for the Christian Life.*)*

SILENCE AND SOLITUDE . . .
FOR THE PURPOSE OF GODLINESS
Explanation of Silence and Solitude
The Discipline of silence is the voluntary and temporary abstention from speaking so that certain spiritual goals might be sought. Sometimes silence is observed in order to read, write, pray, and so on. Though there is no outward speaking, there are internal dialogues with self and with God. This can be called "outward silence." At other times silence is maintained not only outwardly but also inwardly so that God's voice might be heard more clearly.

Solitude is the Spiritual Discipline of voluntarily and temporarily withdrawing to privacy for spiritual purposes. The period of solitude may last only a few minutes or for days. As with silence, solitude may be sought in order to participate without interruption in other Spiritual Disciplines, or just to be alone with God.

First, think of silence and solitude as complementary Disciplines to fellowship. Without silence and solitude we're shallow. Without fellowship we're stagnant. Balance requires them all. Second, silence and solitude are usually found together. Third, recognize that Western culture conditions us to be comfortable with noise and crowds, not with silence and solitude.

There are many biblical reasons for making priorities of the Spiritual Disciplines of silence and solitude:

- To follow Jesus' example. He regularly practiced silence and solitude. (See Matthew 4:1, 14:23; Mark 1:35; Luke 4:42.)
- To hear the voice of God better by getting away from distracting earthly noise and human voices. (See 1 Kings 19:11-13, Galatians 1:17.)
- To express worship to God in a way that does not require words, sounds, or actions. (See Habakkuk 2:20, Zephaniah 1:7.)
- To express faith in God. (See Psalm 62:1-2,5-6; Isaiah 30:15.)
- To seek the salvation of the Lord. (See Lamentations 3:25-28.)
- To be physically and spiritually restored. (See Mark 6:31.)
- To regain a spiritual perspective. (See Luke 1:5-25, 57-64.)
- To seek the will of God, for at times He discloses it only in private. (See Luke 6:12-13.)
- To learn control of the tongue. (See Proverbs 17:27-28; Ecclesiastes 3:7; James 1:19,26, 3:2.) *(Taken from chapter 10 of* Spiritual Disciplines for the Christian Life.)**⁹⁹**

Fasting Explained

4. List the biblical purposes of fasting.

5. Review the various kinds of fasts mentioned in the Bible. Then determine which kind of fast each of the following passages describes:

Deuteronomy 9:9

Ezra 10:6

Esther 4:16

Daniel 1:12

Jonah 3:5-8

Matthew 3:4

Matthew 4:2

Luke 4:2

6. Consider these passages, noticing the word *when*:
   Matthew 6:2-3,5-7,16-17. What do they reveal about the
   importance of fasting?

7. What do we learn about fasting from Matthew 9:14-15?

8. What specific instructions about fasting are given in
   Matthew 6:16-18?

Fasting Is to Be Done for a Purpose

9. Read Ezra 7:11-20, 8:21-23. What was Ezra's situation, and what did he do?

10. God is always pleased to hear His people's prayers and is also pleased when we choose to strengthen our prayers through fasting. Why did the following people fast?

    Nehemiah (Nehemiah 1:4)

    The early Christians (Acts 13:3)

11. What does Judges 20:18-28 teach us about the purpose of fasting?

12. What is the relationship between repentance and fasting? (1 Samuel 7:6, Joel 2:12, Jonah 3:5-8)

13. What does Isaiah 58:6-7 reveal about the role of fasting in meeting the needs of others?

Explanation of Silence and Solitude

14. Look up these verses: Matthew 4:1, 14:23; Mark 1:35; Luke 4:42. What do they tell us about Jesus?

15. Why do you think many of us are uncomfortable when we are alone with our own thoughts and God's voice?

16. Read Mark 6:31. Do you receive enough physical and spiritual rest? What steps can you take to have time alone with God to restore your body and spirit?

17. In which area(s) do you need to discern God's will? What can you learn from Jesus' actions in Luke 6:12-13?

CLOSING PRAYER

Psalm 62:1-2,5-6 contains some beautiful phrases that relate to our faith. Read these verses and write out your thoughts in the form of a prayer. If you, or others, are comfortable praying aloud, do so.

GOING DEEPER
(Extra questions for further study)

18. Are you willing to put aside your physical needs in order to seek God? Why, or why not?

19. Fasting can be little more than a "dead work" if we persistently harden our hearts to God's call to deal with a specific sin in our lives. What sin in your life do you need to deal with today?

20. Consider the following ways you can make silence and solitude more of a reality and a habit. Which will you pursue this coming week?

- Looking to Christ and listening to His Spirit during various "minute retreats" each day.
- Developing a daily time of daily Bible intake and prayer when you're alone with God.
- Experiencing extended periods of silence and solitude—an afternoon, evening, or weekend.
- Locating special places where you can apply the Disciplines of silence and solitude—a park, by a stream, in a special room at home, at church, or elsewhere.
- Asking your spouse or friend to temporarily assume your responsibilities so you can be alone with God.

JOURNALING AND LEARNING ...FOR THE PURPOSE OF GODLINESS

CENTRAL IDEA

Journaling, although not commanded in Scripture, is certainly modeled there. God has blessed the use of journals since biblical times. The Spiritual Discipline of journaling has a fascinating appeal to many people. It not only promotes spiritual growth but is a valuable aid to many other aspects of the spiritual life. Although there are no rules for keeping a journal and journaling can be fruitful at any level of involvement, journaling requires persistence through the dry times. Its value can be experienced only through doing it.

Godly learning is an important Spiritual Discipline because biblically balanced Christians have full heads as well as full hearts. As Proverbs 9:9 tells us, a characteristic of wise people is their desire for godly learning. We must not be content to have zeal without knowledge. Jesus Himself told us to "love the Lord your God . . . with all your mind" (Mark 12:29-30). We glorify God when we use our minds as well as our hearts to learn of Him, His ways, His Word, and His world.

1. Is your impression of journaling positive or negative? What has helped to shape this impression?

2. Why is it important for Christians to continue to learn about God? About the world? About themselves?

JOURNALING . . . FOR THE PURPOSE OF GODLINESS
"More than almost any other Discipline, journaling has a fascinating appeal with nearly all who hear about it. One reason is the way journaling blends biblical doctrine and daily living, like the confluence of two great rivers, into one. Although the practice of journaling is not commanded in Scripture, it is modeled there. And God has blessed the use of journals since biblical times.

Explanation of Journaling
As a Christian, your journal is a place to record the works and ways of God in your life. Your journal also can include an account of daily events, a diary of personal relationships, a notebook of insights into Scripture, and a list of prayer requests. It is where spontaneous devotional thoughts or lengthy theological musings can be preserved.

A journal is one of the best places for charting your progress in the other Spiritual Disciplines and for holding yourself accountable to your goals. Woven throughout this fabric of entries and events are the colorful strands of your reflections and feelings about them. How you respond to these matters, and how you interpret them from your own spiritual perspective, are also at the heart of journaling.

The Bible itself contains many examples of God-inspired journals. Many psalms are records of David's personal spiritual journey with the Lord. We call the journal of Jeremiah's feelings about the fall of Jerusalem the book of Lamentations.

Value of Journaling
Using a journal not only promotes spiritual growth by means of its own virtues, but it's a valuable aid to many other

aspects of the spiritual life. Consider what journaling has to offer in these areas:

Help in self-understanding and evaluation. One of the ways the "progress or decline of the inner man" can be noted through journaling is by the observation of patterns in your life you've not seen before. When I review my journal entries for a month, six months, a year, I see myself and events more objectively. I can analyze my thoughts and actions apart from the feelings I had at the time. From that perspective it's easier to observe whether I've made spiritual progress or have back-slidden in a particular area.

Used appropriately, a journal can actually become a means of propelling us into action for others. The journal can be a mirror in the hands of the Holy Spirit in which He reveals His perspective on our attitudes, thoughts, words, and actions. Since we will be held accountable for each of these at the Judgment, evaluating them by *any* means is wisdom.

Help in meditation. It seems as though more Christians are interested in biblical meditation (cf. Joshua 1:8, Psalm 1:1-3) than ever before. However, meaningful meditation requires a concentration not often developed in our fast-paced, media-distracted society. Sitting with pen and paper heightens my expectation of hearing from God as I think on Him and His words in the passage before me. When I record in a journal my meditations on a passage of Scripture, I can follow more closely the still, small voice of God as He speaks through the text.

Help in expressing thoughts and feelings to the Lord. A journal is a place where we can give expression to the fountain of our heart, where we can unreservedly pour out our passion before the Lord. By slowing us down and prompting us to *think* more deeply about God, journaling helps us *feel* more deeply (and biblically) about God.

Help in remembering the Lord's works. Many people think God has not blessed them with much until they have to move it all to a new address! In the same way, we tend to forget just how many times God has answered specific prayers, made timely provision, and done marvelous things in our lives. Having a journal in which to collect all these memories prevents their being forgotten.

Help in creating and preserving a spiritual heritage.

Journaling is an effective way of teaching the things of God to our children and transmitting our faith into the future (cf. Deuteronomy 6:4-7, 2 Timothy 1:5). We may never know the future spiritual impact of something we write today.

Help in clarifying and articulating insights and impressions. I've discovered that if I write down the meditations of my quiet time with the Lord, those impressions stay with me much longer. Without journaling, by day's end I usually can remember little from my devotional time.

Help in monitoring goals and priorities. A journal is a good way to keep before us the things we want to do and emphasize. Some put a list of goals and priorities in their journal and review it every day.

Help in maintaining the other Spiritual Disciplines. My journal is the place where I record my progress with all the Spiritual Disciplines. Recording the joys and freedom I experience through the Spiritual Disciplines is another way journaling helps maintain my involvement with them. The Christian life is, by definition, a living thing. If we can think of the Discipline of Bible intake as its food and prayer as its breath, many Christians have made journaling its heart. For them it pumps life-maintaining blood into every Discipline connected with it.

Ways of Journaling

How is it done? "Your way of keeping a journal is the right way. . . . There are no rules for keeping a journal!"[1] Many Christians find that the most practical approach is to use everyday notebook paper. While some prefer a spiral-bound notebook and others prefer a preprinted journal book, I find loose-leaf pages more workable. Some feel strongly about only journaling by hand, that it's more spontaneous and expressive. I find that the speed of the word processor or the typewriter actually allows me more freedom of expression than does writing script.

As a starting entry for each day, try listing the one verse or idea from your Bible reading that impressed you most. Meditate on that for a few minutes, then record your insights and impressions. From there consider adding recent events in your life and your feelings and responses to them, brief prayers, joys, successes, failures, quotations, etc. Consider journaling, not only for the purpose of Godliness, but also as a way to raise up a monument of God's faithfulness in your life. *(Taken from chapter 11 of* Spiritual Disciplines for the Christian Life.*)*

LEARNING . . . FOR THE PURPOSE OF GODLINESS

Why do many Christians live as though they've been told, "Choose you this day whom you will serve: scholarship or devotion"? I maintain that a biblically balanced Christian has both a full head and a full heart, radiating both spiritual light and heat. Christians must realize that just as a fire cannot blaze without fuel, so burning hearts are not kindled by brainless heads. We must not be content to have zeal without knowledge.

Does this mean we must be brilliant to be Christians? Absolutely not. But it does mean that to be like Jesus we must be learners even as He was at only age twelve, "sitting among the teachers, listening to them and asking them questions" (Luke 2:46). An examination of the word *disciple* reveals that it means to be not only a "follower" of Christ but also a "learner."

In Proverbs 10:14 we're told, "Wise men store up knowledge." The Hebrew word here means to store up like a treasure. Wise men and women love to learn because they realize that knowledge is like a precious treasure. They not only "acquire" knowledge, they "seek" it.

In Proverbs 23:12, we're commanded, "Apply your heart to instruction and your ears to words of knowledge." No matter how much we know, especially about God, Christ, the Bible, and the Christian life, we still need to apply our heart to learn, for we haven't learned it all.

Fulfilling the Greatest Commandment

Part of what Jesus said was God's greatest commandment is, "Love the Lord your God . . . with all your mind" (Mark 12:29-30). What God wants most from you is your love. And one of the ways He wants you to show love and obedience to Him is by Godly learning. God is glorified when we use the mind He made to learn of Him, His ways, His Word, and His world. Unless we love God with a growing mind, we will be like Christian versions of the Samaritans to whom Jesus said, "You Samaritans worship what you do not know" (John 4:22).

Learning—Essential for Increased Godliness

How is it that we are to be transformed into Christlikeness? The Bible indicates that one of the crucial elements in the process is learning when it says, "Do not conform any longer to the pattern of this world, but be *transformed* by the renewing of your mind" (Romans 12:2, emphasis mine). Growth in Godliness involves a mental renewal that cannot happen without learning. We will not *grow* much in Godliness if we do not know much of what it means to be Godly. We will not become more like Christ if we don't know more of what Christ is like. The Word of God must go through our head if it's going to change our heart and our life.

Learning Is Mostly by Discipline, Not by Accident

We must not assume that we have learned true wisdom just by growing older. The observation found in Job 32:9 is, "The abundant in years may not be wise" (NASB). Age and experience alone don't increase our spiritual maturity. Becoming like Jesus doesn't happen incidentally or automatically with the passing of birthdays. Godliness, as 1 Timothy 4:7 says, requires a deliberate discipline. The Discipline of learning helps us to be *intentional* learners, not accidental learners.

Learn in a Variety of Ways

- Listen to recorded books.
- Listen to cassette tapes.
- Watch Christian videotapes.
- Listen to the radio Bible teaching programs of reputable ministers.
- Arrange to dialogue meaningfully with spiritually mature Christians.
- Read the best books.

Above all, learning has a goal. The goal is Christlikeness. Jesus said in Matthew 11:28-29, "Come to me, all you who are weary and burdened, and I will give you rest. Take my yoke upon you, and *learn* from *me*" (emphasis mine). There is a false or superficial knowledge that "puffs up" (1 Corinthians 8:1), but Godly learning leads to Godly living. *(Taken from chapter 12 of* Spiritual Disciplines for the Christian Life.)**"**

Value of Journaling

3. Why is it important to record the works and ways of God in your life?

Discuss the benefits of journaling in order to chart your progress in the other Spiritual Disciplines. If you have journaled and are willing to do so, share with the group some of what you discovered.

4. How might journaling aid you in doing what Romans 12:3 tells us to do? In biblical meditation?

5. Read Psalm 77:11-12. Which "deeds of the Lord" should you write down and preserve?

6. What do we learn about creating and preserving a spiritual heritage from these verses?

Deuteronomy 6:4-7

2 Timothy 1:5

7. Why is self-accountability so important in our Christian walk?

8. Why is journaling important even when you don't feel like doing it?

9. What type of journal format would be most suitable for you? Why?

The Value of Learning

10. Have you ever known a Christian who deliberately chose not to learn new things? Or one who sought learning continually? What did you observe about each?

11. What is your personal view of the importance of seeking wisdom and knowledge? What do the following passages say about this? (Proverbs 9:9, 10:14, 18:15, 23:12)

12. How does Mark 12:29-30 help you to better understand the importance of Godly learning?

13. In Romans 12:2, what does God call us to do?

Learning Is Mostly by Discipline, Not by Accident

14. Do you agree that those "who are not trying to learn will only get spiritual and biblical knowledge by accident or convenience"? Explain your answer.

15. What role do you think parents play in teaching their children to become intentional learners?

16. Review the ways in which you can learn intentionally. Which ones might help you this week?

17. Are "growing Christians reading Christians"? Why, or why not?

18. What is offered in Proverbs 13:4 to intentional, disciplined learners who seek knowledge and wisdom in order to love God more and become more Christlike?

CLOSING PRAYER

Ask God to help you cultivate a desire for learning more about Him and His Word and to realize the importance of journaling in that process. Thank Him for providing His Word, in which we can discover His truths, and for giving us the Holy Spirit to teach us.

GOING DEEPER
(Extra questions for further study)

19. What changes are you willing to make in order to create the opportunity to journal regularly?

20. What steps will you take this week to learn more about God and what it means to be Godly?

21. If you are a parent, what will you do to help your child(ren) learn intentionally about God and His Word?

22. What price are you willing to pay to become a more disciplined, intentional learner rather than an accidental and by convenience learner?

NOTE
1. Ronald Klug, *How to Keep a Spiritual Journal* (Nashville, TN: Thomas Nelson, 1982), page 58.